WHAT PEOPLE AR̶̶̶ ̶̶̶̶̶̶̶̶̶A̶B̶O̶U̶T̶
THE TENSION OF REDEMPTION . . .

The story of Joe Anderson's life seems unbelievable, except that over the years, I've had a front row seat to watch it happen. His life-altering (and sometimes shocking) challenges, and his transparency about his struggles to face them, encourage anyone who's ever suffered hardship . . . and especially, those who are facing it now. You will be captivated by the drama and challenged to trust God with the circumstances in front of you.

> **Mark Dean**
> **Superintendent, Assemblies of God**
> **Minnesota District Council**

Joe's journey is one of the most powerful, riveting, dramatic, and redemptive stories of grace I have ever encountered. You cannot read this book without reconnecting with the God who relentlessly chases us to affirm His love and purposes. Whether you are experiencing the tragedies of brokenness or the triumphs of grace, you will find inspiration and renewed hope, and you will close the book more in awe of Jesus. With candid honesty, fast-paced storytelling, and characteristic humility, Joe walks us closer to the Master who is the author of all our stories.

> **Ryan Skoog**
> **President / Co-Founder, Venture.org**
> **Burnsville, Minnesota**

Have you ever wanted to give up? Throw in the towel? Walk away from your faith because it seemed like God was distant or at least disinterested in your situation? At one time or another, most of us have experienced this "dark night of the soul." My friend Joe Anderson faced a barrage of dark nights, and yet, he didn't give up on God. Perhaps more importantly, he was keenly aware that God hadn't given up on him.

Joe's story is full of HOPE, and I believe it will inspire and challenge you to cling to God . . . especially in your toughest seasons.

Cory Demmel
Lead Pastor, Cape Christian
Cape Coral, Florida

My friend Joe seems to have lived a hundred lives, and each of them gives us a picture of hope in a trustworthy God. If you want to be ready for life's most perplexing seasons that can be disappointing, dark, and consuming, then follow Joe and Jen's story and find yourself laughing, crying, and growing past the pain with them. This book will give you courage to endure whatever you're facing because God is good.

Dave Simerson
Lead Pastor, Cornerstone Church
Austin, Minnesota

I had the privilege to watch the Anderson's story unfold, so Joe and Jen aren't just names in the news or in a novel. I've seen their struggles, and I've seen their persevering faith in God. It is a poignant and beautiful story. In this book, Joe is opening the door to his heart and inviting us into the heartaches and hopes of their unforgettable experience. If you are going through hardship, do yourself a favor and read this book. From the first page until the last, you won't be able to put it down!

Jeff Grenell
Director, institute for Next Gen (iNG)
Next Gen Specialist, North Central University
Minneapolis, Minnesota

Have you ever felt "Why me?" or "What's next?" From time to time, all of us have felt this way, and we may have asked, "How can I survive this?" Joe Anderson can relate to these questions because he has asked them himself. God's answers weren't always what he expected, and they didn't come as soon as he hoped, but He came through again and again. And now, Joe shares the wisdom he learned from his first-hand experience. Joe has the unique gift set to be able to communicate in a way that not only resonates with our hearts but also gives tangible, street-level directions so we don't just survive . . . we THRIVE! Through faith in Jesus Christ, Joe stands tall and strong today, helping others to be overcomers and conquerors as we apply the lessons of his story to our lives today! Enjoy this fascinating and life-changing read!

Tom Truszinski
CEO, Minnesota Adult & Teen Challenge
www.mntc.org

Joe Anderson's story is both jaw-dropping and inspiring. He has an ability to connect with all audiences through his pain, but then uplift our faith in ways no one else can. Our church was mesmerized and energized when he shared his story with us . . . and you will be too!

Peter Haas
Lead Pastor, Substance Church
Minneapolis, Minnesota
www.substancechurch.com

A MEMOIR

THE
TENSION
OF
REDEMPTION

FROM TRUE CRIME TO TRUE HOPE (AND EVERYTHING IN BETWEEN)

JOE ANDERSON

Scripture citations are from the New American Standard Bible®, Copyright © 1960, 1971,
1977, 1995, 2020 by The Lockman Foundation.
All rights reserved.

ISBNs:
Print: 978-1-947505-60-5
eBook versions: 978-1-947505-61-2

Cover design and interior formatting by Anne McLaughlin,
Blue Lake Design

Published by Baxter Press, Friendswood, Texas

Printed in the United States

CONTENTS

This is my story. It's not meant to be a theological or doctrinal treatise. It's an honest account of my life, not a "how-to" manual. Far from it. In fact, I've made more than my share of mistakes, and I'd do a lot of things differently. I hope that sharing my pain will somehow be your gain.

That's my prayer. Jesus always redeems.

Author's note: In some cases, names and details have been changed to protect anonymity.

FOREWORD

As you read this book, you will become engulfed in the story and—probably at several points—wonder, *Did that really happen?* My wife Becca and I had an "up close and personal" view of almost every event Joe describes in this book, and we can say without reservation, "Yes, it really is true! It really happened."

In fact, I joked with Joe that my foreword could begin and end with one statement: "IT'S ALL TRUE!" But I wanted to write more than that because the Andersons are special people. Becca and I love them very much.

I don't want to steal anything from their story by pointing out some of the twists and turns, but I want to encourage you to "embrace the wow" as you read it. Time after time, Joe and Jen faced insurmountable odds, death, tragedy, heartache, betrayal, foolish assumptions, unexpected detours, shattered hearts, and a shattered body—it was everything life could throw at them. It's an astounding story. (Honestly, you may think some of it has to be made up, but I assure you it's true—it really happened!)

As a pastor, I've experienced my own set of heartaches, and I've been with people who have suffered a wide range of difficulties. Some of the problems have been self-inflicted, some are at the hands of people they trusted but betrayed them, and some are unforeseen and unexpected calamities caused by a traffic accident or a natural disaster. In all of these, our first question is often, "Why? Why, God, did You allow this to happen?" That's not the wrong question, but we often don't listen for His answer. James, the half-brother of Jesus and the leader of the church in Jerusalem in the years after Jesus was crucified and raised from the grave, wrote people who were struggling, "Consider it pure joy, my brothers and sisters, whenever you face trials of many kinds, because you know that the testing of your faith produces perseverance. Let perseverance finish its work so that you may be mature and complete, not lacking anything" (James 1:2-4). When we learn to view our difficulties, whatever the cause, as a trial—a test to deepen our faith in a wise and loving God—we'll still hurt, but we'll have assurance there's purpose in our pain.

When we read the Bible, we see biographies of men and women who experienced life-shaking heartaches, opposition, cruelty, and other kinds of suffering. God's purpose wasn't to beat them down and cause them to lose their faith. His purpose was to build their faith and make them examples of resilient hope in God's love, power, and leading. The issue is perspective. Oswald Chambers observed, "We all know people who have been made much meaner and more irritable and more intolerable to live with by suffering: it is not right to say that all suffering perfects. It only perfects one type of person—the one who accepts the call of God in Christ Jesus."

That's the story of Joe and Jen's journey of faith. Through it all, they accepted God's call.

As you read each chapter, let their story inspire you, bring you hope, and compel you to stop and thank God for their resilience. Follow their example to keep fighting the good fight and keep believing in a God who loves us even when we feel unlovable and who keeps His promises even when it seems we've hit a dead end.

Get ready, you've never heard a story like this, and I need to say it one more time, it's true: It really happened! Dive in, and when you're done, you'll be so glad that Joe shared this incredible story with all of us, and you'll be filled with faith to face anything that the world will throw at you!

Rob Ketterling
Lead Pastor, River Valley Church
Burnsville, Minnesota
www.rivervalley.org

CHAPTER 1
SHOTGUN WEDDING

I was startled by the phone ringing on the nightstand just inches from my head. It took a few seconds to realize where I was. I was in a hotel room . . . and there was someone next to me. Oh, yeah. Jen and I had gotten married the night before, and I was waking up next to the girl of my dreams. I glanced at the clock. It read 5:56 a.m.

Instantly, I concluded the hotel had messed up the wakeup call . . . and then I wondered if my groomsmen were pranking me again. I picked up the phone and heard Christa, Jen's sister-in-law, who was trying to communicate through screams and sobs. It wasn't what I was expecting at all. I could understand, though, that she was asking to speak to Jen. I tapped Jen on the shoulder to wake her up. When she turned over, I said, "Jen, something's wrong" and handed her the phone.

I wondered if one of her relatives who had been at the wedding had been in an accident. Jen listened for just a few seconds, and then she reacted, "Oh no! Oh no! Oh no!" She dropped the phone and started running around the room. She was in shock. She kept saying, "Jesus, no! Jesus, no! This can't be happening! It can't be real!"

I picked up the phone to ask Christa what had happened. All I really understood was that Jen's father had been shot and was on the way to the hospital.

Before I tell the rest of what happened that day, let me take you back to the day before.

October 26, 1996 was a beautiful day in Milford, Michigan. Jen and I had been looking forward to our wedding day for a long time, and it had finally arrived. She had been living at her parents' home during the summer. Her father loves everybody and everybody loves him. He is a well-known and respected pastor in the community, with a reputation for hugging and praying for every person he encountered, whether they were members of his church or not. He was going to walk his daughter down the aisle and then officiate in the ceremony along with my friend and pastor from the Twin Cities, Rob Ketterling. In fact, Pastor Rob is more like the big brother I'd always wanted. Jen's parents, Bill and JoAnne Peppard, are wonderful people. Milford is the quintessential small community, fairly upscale, with close bonds because people are very much involved in each other's lives.

Jen and I had gone to school at North Central University in Minneapolis, and over the summer leading up to the wedding, I'd been living at my parents' home south of metro Minneapolis, finishing my senior project so I could graduate the next spring. I was working as a bill collector while interning at River Valley Church. With my groomsmen and ushers, we made the twelve-hour trip to Milford on Friday, the day before the wedding.

At the rehearsal party, people in the bridal party told stories about Jen and me. It couldn't have been more fun. Jen and I treasured our relationships with all of them. Our parents beamed as they listened to it all. That night, the bridesmaids and groomsmen gathered at Jen's parents' house for a bonfire.

After the rehearsal dinner, I went back to the hotel with my groomsmen. They had been waiting for this moment to take revenge on me for some of the pranks I'd played on them when they got married. My friends and I have a very strong bond, and we've developed more than a few strange traditions. It all started when the first of us got married, and the rest of the guys decided that hazing would be entirely appropriate, including various forms of good-natured torture and embarrassing him in front of his bride-to-be. I was next on the hit list. At the hotel, they grabbed me, stripped off my clothes, wrote notes to Jen on my chest and back with markers, and put me in thermal underwear like a prisoner's jumpsuit. Then they put me in the trunk of the car.

The first stop was at a store where they bought supplies. They left me in the trunk with the engine running, and the exhaust fumes wafted into the trunk. I'm glad they came out pretty quickly to let me get some fresh air or it could have been a short night for me! By this time, it was close to midnight. They drove back to Jen's parents' house, opened the trunk, duct-taped me to a lawn chair facing her parents' front porch, and shined the car lights on the front door. They honked the horns so Jen, her bridesmaids, and her parents would come out. They told Jen that she had to answer sports trivia questions . . . and for every wrong answer, I'd pay a price. Of course, they asked her about things she had no clue how to answer: How many Super Bowls have the Vikings won? She said "Three," but of course, they've never won it. (That one always stings.) Who's the starting quarterback for the Vikings? She said "Joe Montana," who had played for the 49ers. Who's the starting running back? She said "Walter Payton," who had played for the Chicago Bears. She got them *all* wrong! After each one, the guys did their dirty work: they poured a gallon of cold milk on me, pummeled me with eggs, and poured pancake batter over me. The eggs really hurt. It was like being hit with golf balls. By the end of their version of *Jeopardy* with Jen, I was barely recognizable. The bridesmaids from Michigan, who didn't really know me or my friends, were shocked that they would do this to me, but the ones from our college told them, "Of all people, Joe has this coming to him!" The guys hosed me down with freezing cold water, threw me back in the trunk, and as I shivered, drove back to the hotel. Sometimes guys might wonder if they really need a shower . . . this wasn't one of those times.

When I got up that Saturday morning and looked outside, it was one of the most beautiful autumn days I'd ever seen. The air was crisp and clear, the sky was bright blue, and the leaves were in their full color. What a day to marry the girl of my dreams!

After breakfast, the guys and I wanted to blow off a little steam before the ceremony, so we played football. It was a lot of fun, especially getting to know Jen's brother Greg, who tackled me hard even though we were playing touch football—I guess that's what older brothers do! But I had a major problem: I needed the skills of a United Nations ambassador because the New York Yankees were playing Game 6 of the World Series that night. It was Derek Jeter's first Series, and my guys didn't want to miss it. If they had been umpires, they would have given me an error on my scheduling of the wedding.

That afternoon, the church was filled with smiling people. pretty dresses, tuxes, flowers—the whole thing. I stood next to my best man, Ryan Ketterling (Pastor Rob's younger brother). As I watched the rear doors open and saw Jen's dad walk her down the aisle, I was thrilled—she was more beautiful than ever!

Jen looked absolutely stunning. I could hardly believe she was willing to marry me. Guys who know us often tell me something like, "Man, when you married her, you outkicked your coverage!" They're exactly right. She was (and is) ridiculously stunning: dark hair, greenish-blue eyes, great smile. In fact, people often stopped her on the street or in stores to tell her she looked exactly like a young, beautiful Elizabeth Taylor. As Jen and her father approached the front of the church, I saw that he was very emotional. Everybody who knew Bill fully expected this reaction because he's such a soft-hearted crier and loves Jen so much. (Bets were made that he wouldn't be able to speak at all through his tears during the ceremony.) This was almost as big a day for Bill as it was for Jen. He was smiling and crying at the same time. He gave me Jen's hand and walked around to face us and the audience.

The ceremony was a blur of words and emotions, but through it all, I was overcome with the reality that I was getting married to the most beautiful, wonderful woman on the planet. Waves of joy and gratitude swept over me. The future couldn't have looked brighter—in every area of my life.

We were pronounced "husband and wife." I know the exact moment because a friend looked at his watch and wrote the time on a business card:

"Mr. and Mrs. Joseph Anderson, 6:39:50 p.m., October 26, 1996." Jen and I kissed, and we walked down the aisle to the cheers of all our family and friends. The reception was at the church. I don't remember much about the meal, but I'm sure it was delicious and everybody had a great time. As I told this part of the story, a friend asked if we had a dance at the church. I told him, "You've got to be kidding! This was old-school Assemblies of God! We were taught to avoid drinking, drugs, and premarital sex because they might lead to dancing!"

As the night went on, people said their goodbyes and began to leave. After a while, Jen and I gathered up all the presents and cards. It dawned on me that when you marry a pastor's daughter, you make out really well with gifts! We took them to Bill and JoAnne's house a little way down the road, and put them in the living room. The plan was for Jen and me to spend our first night together at the hotel and then come back the next morning to open presents. We had a flight on Sunday afternoon for our honeymoon in Florida.

As I drifted off to sleep later that night, I felt euphoric. The day couldn't have gone better—the friends, the weather, the ceremony, and the woman I love lying next to me. Almost heaven! I set the alarm for 8:30 the next morning.

Sometime in the night, a cold front swept through the area with a powerful wind that blew most of the leaves off the trees, leaving a fog more dense than I've ever seen. The scene had changed from one of the most beautiful days to a setting for a horror movie. But of course, Jen and I didn't know it yet. We had fallen asleep in a dreamworld, but we woke up to our worst nightmare.

And now, back to the morning of the shooting.

After Jen got off the phone, we wanted to get to the hospital as soon as possible. I rushed into the bathroom. Should I shave? Should I put on deodorant? Should I take a shower? I wasn't sure how to respond . . . because I'd never been in any situation like this before! It felt almost like an out-of-body experience, as if I were watching myself from above in a movie scene, trying to decide what my character should be doing right now, as if each movement and moment had huge significance. I brushed my teeth, put on deodorant, and threw on a pair of jeans and a hoodie. Jen put her coat on over her pajamas, and we rushed out of the room. I remember looking at my tuxedo and thinking, *When will I get time to return it?* Then I felt guilty for even thinking that. My mind was scrambled. We sped to the hospital.

This is what we learned: At about 5:00 that morning in the darkness and thick fog, a man had come to the house. It's about a quarter of a mile down a dirt driveway from the church—a beautiful new two-story home on three acres with a walkout basement in the back. The man walked past the firepit where we'd had the bonfire two nights before, cut the phone line, and entered the unfinished basement of Jen's parents' house. He went up the stairs to the main level of the house, turned on all the lights, and unlocked all the doors so he could choose any of them for his escape. Strangely, he also turned on all the lights in the garage.

Jen's mom and dad weren't alone in the house. Her two teenage sisters, Jodi and Leah, were there, as well as two elderly women who needed a place to stay. That wasn't unusual for the Peppards. They're very gracious and generous. In fact, the basement was being prepared for home health care for Jen's mom, who is a nurse, to care for people like these ladies. The family also had two small inside dogs. For several days, Jen's bridal party had stayed at the house. It had been a hive of activity all week, but they had left after the reception.

All of the gifts and cards, most with cash in them, were in the middle of the living room in plain sight, but the man didn't touch any of them—he wasn't there to rob Bill and JoAnne. He walked up the stairs to the second story where there are two bedrooms: one for Jen's parents and the other for her sisters.

He opened the door to Bill and JoAnne's bedroom, turned on the lights, and walked to JoAnne's side of the bed. When she opened her eyes, she saw a large man wearing a ski mask and holding a 12-gauge shotgun. She hoped this was just a terrible dream, but it wasn't like any she'd ever had before. She closed her eyes and began praying. By this time, Bill was waking up. He rolled over on his left side to get a better view of what was going on. The man was pointing the barrel of the gun past JoAnne and directly toward his chest. He leaned on his left elbow and held out his right hand and yelled, "No!" The end of the barrel was about two feet from his chest.

The blast of the gun was deafening. The shotgun wasn't loaded with birdshot: it held a slug, a solid mass of lead the diameter of the 12-gauge barrel, much larger than the bullet of any normal rifle. It blew a softball-sized hole in Bill's chest. The slug went out his back, through the wall, and into the yard.

Bill was writhing and bleeding. Blood was everywhere—on the wall, the floor, the bed, and of course, on him. The man never said a word. He just turned and ran out of the bedroom, down the stairs, out a door, and into the fog.

Jodi and Leah wondered if the blast and the sound of footsteps down the stairs was another prank the guys were playing, but it didn't make sense that they would play one on Jen's parents. They ran into the bedroom and witnessed the horrific sight. Their father was covered in blood and writhing in the bed.

JoAnne told them to call 9-1-1. Eighteen-year-old Jodi quickly dialed the number, but all she heard was silence. They tried every phone in the house. Nothing. (This was before cell phones, so that wasn't an option.) You can imagine the sheer terror they felt—they had no way of knowing the phone line was cut. They just knew the phones wouldn't work. Where would they find help? Where was the shooter? Was he hiding in the house? Their imaginations ran wild. It was a horrific nightmare.

As a nurse, JoAnne instantly assessed Bill's condition, and she could see that he was going to die if he didn't get help really soon. And even then . . .

She grabbed a towel and told Leah to press it over the wound on her father's chest. Leah had just turned seventeen earlier that month. She was going through some difficult times with teenage angst and rebellion. Now, as she stood over her father, she wept. She was screaming and pleading with him, "Don't die, Daddy! I need you in my life, Daddy! Please don't die!" Bill felt his life ebbing away, and he could only look into her eyes and whisper what he thought were his final words to her: "Serve Jesus. Serve Jesus. Serve Jesus."

Jodi got into a car and drove to the church to call from there, but no one knew if the intruder was still nearby. She grabbed a golf club in case she had to defend herself. When she approached the church, she saw a light was on inside. She sensed the Holy Spirit warn her not to go in, so she drove about a mile to the house of a neighbor who was a 9-1-1 operator. When she came to the door, Jodi blurted out the horrific news, and the neighbor called the police. In only a few minutes, officers arrived at Jen's parents' house. The neighbor asked Jodi to stay with her because she was obviously in shock.

Paramedics arrived a few minutes later. Initially, they couldn't go in because the house hadn't been cleared by the police, and the shooter hadn't been arrested. The officer who arrived first was a friend of Bill's. (Bill was a volunteer chaplain for the department.) He used very colorful and persuasive language to get the paramedics inside because he knew there was no time to waste. As they worked on Bill, one of their main concerns was the staggering loss of blood. The average person has ten pints, and they estimated that Bill had lost seven. He was a ghostly white. They had trouble stopping the blood. When they put him on a stretcher to carry him down the stairs, he left a waterfall of blood on the steps.

In the ambulance, they planned to take him to one of the larger regional hospitals, but the EMT working on Bill told them, "He's not going to make it if we take that long." They arrived at Huron Valley Hospital and wheeled him into the ER. A skilled surgeon had been called in a few hours earlier to care for people who had been in a car wreck. He was leaving the hospital to go home as the ambulance roared to a stop. He realized that his skills might be needed, so he returned to the ER to see if he could help. He could. He became the lead physician on the team.

In the operating room, the doctor, who wasn't a believer, stopped his preparation and announced, "This is a man of God. Everything is going to be okay." The nurses and technicians had never heard him say anything like this before.

By this time, everyone in the family had found a ride to the hospital. JoAnne and the girls were still in their pajamas and robes—their clothes were still splattered with blood. We immediately huddled together to pray. Shaking and sobbing, the only words that came out were "Jesus, Jesus, Jesus." We began praying in the Spirit out loud. I never fully understood Romans 8:26 until that moment: "We do not know what we ought to pray for, but the Spirit himself intercedes for us through wordless groans." I wanted to get more information so I very gently asked JoAnne what happened. She told me about the man with the long gun. I had been serving in the Air Force, and I'd been trained in firearms, so that didn't make sense to me. If Bill had been shot in the chest with a rifle from close range, I didn't see any way he'd still be alive. The tumbling action of the bullet would have certainly killed him, but he was still clinging to life.

Jen was still in her pajamas, but I noticed that she was wearing the white shoes she'd worn in the wedding. It hit me like a brick: only a few hours before, she had worn those shoes as her dad escorted her down the aisle, and now she was wearing them as he fought for life. I wanted to scream, "How can this be happening?!" But of course, I didn't. I felt totally unprepared for this . . . so inept . . . so immature . . . so helpless. At that moment, I thought of Jesus' parable at the end of the Sermon on the Mount. We can build our lives on the rock or the sand, and when the storms come, we find out if our foundation is firm. I realized much of my life had been, well, sandy. This was a storm I'd never have imagined, and I wondered how I would handle it. Jen and her family needed me to be strong.

The bridal party was staying at a different hotel. I called my grooms-men to give them the bad news. My best man Ryan answered, listened to me for a few seconds, laughed, and hung up. He was sure I was pranking them. I called back, but I still had trouble convincing him that I was seri-ous. But finally, he could hear in my voice that I wasn't kidding. We had served together in the Air Force, and our military training took over. I told him what had happened and that I needed him to try and get me a gun so I could protect all of us. I called Pastor Rob to tell him what had happened. He prayed with me and offered to break the news to my parents. He walked across the hall, knocked on the door, and gave them the tragic news. My mother collapsed to her knees and began to pray.

One of the saddest moments I can remember was when Bill's elderly parents arrived at the hospital. Bill's father was crying and asking no one but everyone, "Why would anyone want to hurt my Billy? Billy loved every-body. Why would anyone shoot my Billy?" It was heart-wrenching to watch him deal with the shock.

Bill had been involved in a number of outreaches and service organiza-tions in the area, so many people were familiar with him and his ministry. This was before social media and email, but still, word of the attack soon spread to pastors around the area, and even across the country and around the world. Thousands were praying for Bill and the family that Sunday morning. Soon, news crews arrived at the hospital. In only a few minutes, the waiting room became crowded with people—many of whom JoAnne and the rest of the family didn't know. We hadn't identified the assailant, and we couldn't be sure he wasn't one of the people near us. Our concerns and fears were very different from the aftermath of a car crash. In those cases, the people who care don't have to wonder if the perpetrator is looking for his next victim . . . or to finish the job on Bill.

The surgeon came to the door and asked to speak to JoAnne. The look on his face wasn't optimistic, so I assumed the worst. Instead, he told us that Bill was alive, but he wasn't out of the woods yet. The slug had missed his vital organs, but it had still caused extensive damage. It would be some time before he'd know if Bill would survive.

The police came and cleared the room. The hospital administrator put the waiting room on lockdown so no visitors would interrupt us. The wedding party showed up and prayed with us. They wanted to help in some way, but we told them there was nothing to do but pray. They couldn't stay at the hospital anyway because of the lockdown.

As the initial fear of Bill's dying began to subside, the fear of the man returning took its place. Why had he come to that house on that night? Why hadn't he taken anything? What could his motive possibly be? Where was he now? As we looked at faces in the hall and later on the street, we wondered, *Could that be him? How about that guy? Or that one?*

That afternoon, Bill was in a medically induced coma, but he was stable. Sometime after five o'clock, Jen and I drove back to her parents' house to get her mother some clothes. I wish someone had told us that wasn't a good idea. It's weird: when you're in shock, you don't realize it, so you can make bad decisions—like our going back to the house by ourselves. When we walked into the living room and started walking up the stairs, all the blood gave us another shock, and we were gripped with anger. I had a strong, terrible metallic taste in my mouth, and I felt like throwing up. When we went to her parents' bedroom, the mattress was pulled almost off the bed. There was so much blood that it was inconceivable that anyone who'd lost that much would still be alive. Jen and I both had increasing levels of shock as we walked through the house. The air felt thick, like it was buzzing with some kind of evil static electricity. Early that morning, we had experienced a rush of adrenaline when we first heard the news about the shooting. During the day, we'd calmed down, but we were still in shock. Now, at the scene of the crime again, it all came rushing back. Jen pounded on the wall and yelled, "I can't believe someone did this to my dad!" Later, I thought of the verse in the opening chapters of Genesis when it says that Abel's blood was crying out from the ground. Bill's blood was crying out for justice.

The sun went down about thirty minutes after we arrived. From the time I woke up that morning, I kept looking at my watch to mark the exact time of each event of the day . . . and how long it had been since our wedding ceremony. I don't know if it was a coping mechanism, but I kept thinking things like, *Now it's been almost twenty-four hours since our ceremony . . . and counting.* The approaching darkness reminded us that we were in a house, alone, with the phone lines still cut, on three acres of property, down a dirt road, and a tangible sense of spiritual darkness seemed to be closing in on us. Both of us were terrified that the man hadn't finished what he started, and we might be next. I told Jen, "We need to get out of here right now!" We grabbed a few things, ran to the car, and sped away.

We went back to the hospital to spend the night with Jen's family. Bill was on the third floor, and the elevator was near the waiting room. All of us tried to sleep, but our night was like one long, intense, collective night terror. Throughout the night, I heard moaning and crying as we all kept falling asleep to only wake up again in fear and shock.

Of course, our minds raced as we tried to make sense of what happened. I wondered if Bill had been threatened, but he didn't tell us because he didn't want anything to break the joyful atmosphere of our wedding. On Monday morning, the police set up an interview room in the hospital to question each family member and people close to the situation. Two detectives sat on one side of the table as Jen and I went in together and sat across from them. They began to pepper us with questions: "Do either of you have an ex-boy-friend or ex-girlfriend?" "Was anyone against you getting married?" "Who was in the wedding party? Where were they all last night?"

We answered all their questions, but then one of them said, "We noticed eggshells in the yard. What's that about?" I tried to explain that my groomsmen had hazed me on Friday night, and they'd thrown eggs at me. They asked for the groomsmen's shoe size so they could see if one of them matched a footprint they found outside the house. The detectives looked at us suspiciously. I know . . . that's their job, but I wanted to yell, "Hey, back off! We're the good guys! We didn't do this!" But of course, I didn't say any of that.

Halloween was later that week, and the ghoulish decorations were already up. I've always disliked Halloween, but during those days I really hated it. People wearing costumes and masks in the hospital and making light of evil. How could they? The only bright spot in the day was that on that night my team, the Minnesota Vikings, played on Monday Night Football against the Chicago Bears. I searched for a television in the hospital and hoped a good win would be a welcome distraction to all the chaos around me. We were favored, but we lost, and to make things worse, our star running back, Robert Smith, got hurt and was lost for the rest of the season. So much for a good distraction, and so much for my fantasy football season.

We were waiting for Bill to wake up so he could shed any light on the situation. Maybe he knew who it was. Maybe he recognized the man even though he was wearing a ski mask and didn't speak a word. Finally, on Tuesday afternoon, Bill woke up. He had a breathing tube, so he motioned for someone to give him a pen and a piece of paper. He wrote, "Family?" The nurses assured him that everyone was okay. From the moment Bill opened his eyes, his main concern was the health and safety of JoAnne, the girls, and the rest of the family. Soon, the breathing tube was removed. When the police questioned him, he told them he had no idea who the man might be, why he'd shot him, and why he didn't steal anything. Even in that short time, Bill's hair had turned from black to almost completely grey. It's a condition called Canities Subita, and is caused by excessive stress or trauma. I thought it happened only in cartoons, but it was real. I understand that can happen in only a few days when the body experiences extreme shock.

The nature of the shooting made it look like a crime of passion. The police began with the assumption that either Bill or JoAnne was having an affair, and the shooter was a rival or an aggrieved spouse. Bill and JoAnne assured the police that this wasn't the case. Bill told them, "If you think I'm lying to cover for someone—who shot me and left me for dead—you need to come up with a better set of assumptions." They were back to square one.

For the first two nights, the police assigned an officer to sit in front of Bill's room for protection, but they didn't have enough manpower for additional nights. I took the night shifts for the next eight days until Bill was released. The room was near the elevators, so I pulled a chair next to them to wait and watch. When I dozed off, I startled awake every time the doors opened. Through my increasingly exhausted glare, I stared at each person exiting the elevator, looking for a long gun or a pistol.

The hospital was being renovated, and the work area was at the opposite end of the hallway from Bill's room. Translucent plastic, wires, and work lights hung from the ceiling. Stacks of drywall and other building supplies were stacked on the floor. Contractor equipment was seemingly everywhere. There must have been a short somewhere in the electrical system because the power went out without warning from time to time. We experienced a couple of seconds of darkness before the backup generator kicked on. Hospitals at night are inherently creepy places, but this was putting it over the top! I would have liked a pristine and safe environment so I could have more peace of mind, but the ongoing construction and periodic blackouts only added to the chaos of the week.

This might sound selfish and petty, but as a red-blooded young man, I had been looking forward to our honeymoon more than any other part of the wedding. For years my Christian friends and I would ask each other the hypothetical question: "If Jesus came back on your wedding night, would you be upset?" My answer was always, "The Bible says 'no mind can conceive what God has prepared for us,' so heaven is hard to imagine. However, my mind has been vividly imagining what my honeymoon would be like since I was about thirteen!" But this situation was worse: no Rapture and no honeymoon. Obviously, the mood wasn't right. I was stuck in marital purgatory, which was a huge disappointment to me.

Some things about the shooting still didn't make sense. Bill had a habit of studying alone at the church late into the night. It would have been very easy for someone to come into the church, kill him, and leave in the dark without anyone noticing. Why had this man chosen to come into a house where JoAnne, the two girls, their dogs, and the two older ladies were living?

As the days in the hospital dragged on, Jen and her mother began to focus on a person they'd known years before. When Jen was fourteen, a man in his mid-twenties attended the church, and he began telling people that God had told him that he would marry Jen . . . and her mother. (I'm not making this up.) As he told more people, they became concerned and told Bill. The man didn't give off any vibes of a personality disorder, but he was obviously delusional. Bill is one of the most gentle, loving pastors you'll ever meet, and he set up a meeting with him. As they sat in Bill's office, Bill calmly confronted him, and he asked for an explanation. Surely, Bill thought, there had been some wild exaggerations and terrible misunderstandings. The man looked at Bill and said plainly, "God told me that I'm going to have your wife and your daughter as my wives. I'll have them sexually and in every other way. You can count on it." There hadn't been any exaggerations.

Bill responded, "This isn't from God. You're deceived, and you need professional help."

He reacted defiantly, "No, I'm sure of it!"

Bill told him that he was no longer welcome at the church. He initially stalked JoAnne and followed her several times to the hospital where she worked. When the police were contacted, it stopped. As far as the family knew, there was no more contact with him over the next seven years. It all fit like a glove: Bill had gotten in the way of his grand plan. If Bill was eliminated, JoAnne would be free to marry. And he chose that day to punish Bill because he had officiated in marrying his daughter to me. That, at least, was a plausible theory.

(The story gets even more bizarre: The police investigated the guy, and his live-in girlfriend gave him an alibi by telling the police that he had been in bed with her all night. The police didn't believe her, but they couldn't prove that she was lying. Years later, she left him, fell in love with another guy, and they began attending church. They got saved. Her family thought her conversion might prompt her to come clean and tell the police about her previous boyfriend's involvement in the shooting, but just days after they went forward and trusted Jesus, she and her boyfriend were found shot to death in their bed. The murder, like Bill's shooting, was never solved. The police and the families were convinced the delusional guy had committed both crimes, but they couldn't find enough evidence to indict him. Bill-boards in the area demanded justice, and a local version of *America's Most Wanted* got involved. Cases like this rarely go unsolved, but this time . . .)

The doctors thought Bill would be in the hospital for at least a month, and maybe longer, but he was released only ten days after the shooting. The surgeon had reconstructed some of his organs, and he removed sections of Bill's intestines, but we considered it to be a miracle that he was alive. No one wanted to go back to the house. Close friends of Bill and JoAnne had a second home, and they offered it to Jen's family for as long as they needed it. We were with them at the house for four days. On one of those afternoons, Jen and I went to pick up the video of the wedding. The police had asked us to review it to make sure the killer hadn't been among all the faces in the crowd. They wanted us to make a list of every person who had attended. On the way back from picking it up, I noticed a car was still following us after there had been many intersections along the road. He made every turn we made. I was sure it was the killer. I told Jen, "I'm not going to lead this guy back to the house. At some point, I may get out of the car. If I do, jump in the driver's seat and get away as fast as you can!" At the next turn, he went straight. I finally realized that the guy was just going home, and it was only a coincidence that he lived somewhere near the safe house. It's amazing what paranoia can do to your mind.

When Jen and I watched the wedding video with her parents, it felt so odd. We were watching the happiest moment of our lives, but it had become a crime scene. We looked at every person in every scene, but no, we didn't identify anyone who didn't belong. Another dead end.

I wondered what was next for Jen and me. Since that Sunday morning, our lives had been turned upside down, just like everyone else in the family. I needed to go back to work, but Jen didn't want to leave her dad. They had always been very close, and now that both of them were traumatized, she wanted to be near him more than ever.

It won't come as a surprise to anyone that this moment created enormous tension between Jen and me. She felt protective of her dad, and she wanted to be near her mother and sisters. She couldn't imagine leaving them with so much left up in the air—especially the nagging fact that the shooter was still out there somewhere, perhaps plotting his next move against her dad and the family. But me? I wanted to get out of there, to begin to put all this behind us so we could rebuild our relationship and plan our future together. To Jen, Milford and her family were home and safety; to me, home was the Twin Cities.

Jen was suffering from survivor's guilt because she hadn't been at home with her mom and her sisters when the man shot her dad. She also felt guilty that it happened on our wedding night, as if it was somehow her fault for getting married. She couldn't stop thinking that if she'd made different decisions, none of this would have happened. Our minds were filled with a flood of what-ifs. Instead of reminiscing about butterfly kisses, she was obsessing about the butterfly effect of our wedding.

Four days after Bill and the family were settled in their temporary home, it was time for Jen and me to leave. She resisted packing at every turn, and the tension between us mounted. Her every nonverbal message screamed at me, "I'd rather be a daughter than a wife!"

Things would only get worse from there.

CHAPTER 2

THE PASTORIZER

A friend who knows a lot of my crazy stories shook his head and said, "Joe, I've known a lot of people, and I can honestly say you're the unluckiest guy I know *and* at the same time, the luckiest guy in the world! No matter what happens with you, something always works out." We don't usually use the word "luck" when we refer to what God is doing, but I knew exactly what he was saying. I've lived this paradox for decades.

Let me back up to describe some important events in my childhood and then explain how Jen and I met and fell in love.

I had the privilege to grow up in a family where Christ is honored and love was sewn into the fabric of daily life. Both sets of my grandparents got saved as young adults in their twenties, and they were excited about living for the Lord and walking a Spirit-filled life. Of course, they brought my parents up to love God , and they were wonderful role models for me. As first-generation believers, they were very concerned about their legacy, so they prayed fervently for my parents, for me, and for everyone else in the family. Sundays were always about church, and in the fall and early winter, watching the Minnesota Vikings. My dad and my grandpa were diehard fans. One of my earliest memories is walking into the living room where my father and grandfather were watching the Vikings on TV. Suddenly, both of them stood up and yelled at the television! I was terrified by their outburst and ran into the room where my grandma and mom were sitting. My grandma calmed me down by telling me, "Don't be afraid. They're not really mad. They're just Vikings fans." That was part of my early discipleship as a true fan of the Vikings.

My mom is the most caring and compassionate person you can ever meet, and my dad is a rock: strong, fun-loving, and always excited about going to work. Every Sunday—and I mean *every* Sunday—as we got ready for church, I saw his tithe check sitting on the table so he could pick it up as we walked out the door. My dad's father and I were very close. I was his only grandson. He had been a hero in World War II, earning two Purple Hearts. Two weeks before I was born, he had a stroke. He was in the same hospital where I was born, and I have a picture of him in his hospital bed holding me. He was permanently paralyzed on his left side, and this somehow created a special bond between us. I think he prayed for me more than anyone else. I remember going over to my grandparents' house and he let me sleep in the bed with him. On those nights, I fell asleep to the sound of my grandpa praying out loud for me with his hand on my head. One night when I woke up and heard him praying, I didn't feel his hand on my head. I looked over and saw that his hand was on my teddy bear's head. He was praying a powerful prayer of blessing. I felt like I was Esau and my teddy bear was Jacob, stealing my grandfather's blessing! (I've often wondered what that teddy bear went on to do for the Lord. I'm sure it's been amazing!)

I trusted in Christ when I was just a boy, and later, on a Saturday morning at a youth retreat, I sensed God's clear call to vocational ministry. The room was so packed that I sat in the choir loft behind the speaker. During the message, the Spirit was working deeply in my heart. I was crying, but I couldn't articulate very well what God was doing. All I knew was that He was calling me to be a pastor. My youth pastor came over and put his arm around me. He asked me what was going on, and as best I could, I told him that I was sure God wanted me to be a pastor. To my surprise, he looked at me and said, "Joe, I can see that in you." His affirmation rang true to me. God's calling in my life wasn't in a vacuum. I'm from a big extended family, and a number of my uncles and other relatives are pastors.

A few months later, my ninth-grade teacher gave our class an assignment to write a paper about what we wanted to do when we grew up. It got a little complicated because, to be completely honest, my heart's desire was to become a professional wrestler. Now I had to figure out how I could be both—a professional wrestler who uses his platform to reach people as a pastor. I had it all planned: On Saturday nights, I'd be the greatest draw in the history of the ring, and on Sunday morning, people would flock to my church to hear me preach.

I loved the wrestlers who had larger-than-life personalities and really cool names, like Jake the Snake Roberts, Ravishing Rick Rude, Rowdy Roddy Piper, and my all-time favorites for their microphone skills, Randy the Macho Man Savage and The Nature Boy Ric Flair—WOOOO!

After a lot of thought, I decided my ring name would be "The Pastor-izer." It combined the ferocity of wrestling (terrorizing opponents) with my

God-given calling (as a pastor). After my fin-ishing move, my opponent would be Pastorized. It was going to be devastating for them and spectacular for me.

Paul was a good friend in high school, and he was into wrestling as much as I was (almost).We spent hours after school practic-ing wrestling moves and choreographing our matches based off the latest drama from the WWF broadcast that week. Eventually, we started performing for friends in the hallway at school. Our act became more and more pop-ular, especially with the upperclassmen, so we kept topping ourselves and getting more daring with our moves. It was a lot of pressure to outdo the performance from the previous week, and we used Paul's room with a bunk bed and a mattress on the floor to practice the high flying moves. It was a miracle we didn't break our necks doing this at school. I was bigger and stronger, and he was small and more agile, so I would throw and give him a body slam, suplex, or pile driver. Paul would hit me with flying double-leg kicks, leg drops, and full slaps to my face and chest. It was a fair and equal division of pain and punishment. After the first couple of times, hundreds of kids came to watch us. Even the teachers must have been entertained because very few of them expressed any concerns.

But one teacher didn't get the memo. One day Paul and I were put-ting on a show—I was pretending to be Brutus the Barber Beefcake. When Brutus knocked out an opponent, he would grab a pair of scissors, cut off a chunk of the guy's hair, and throw it up in the air. We choreographed the move, Paul acted like I'd knocked him out, and I pulled out scissors and pre-tended to cut his hair. Actually, it was a handful I'd cut off my dog the night before. When I threw the hair in the air, the crowd went wild! It was awesome! At that moment, a teacher walked up, saw the scissors, and assumed we were actually fighting and I had a weapon. He hauled us into the principal's office for fighting. I wish you could have heard us try to explain the situation to the principal: "You see, we're best friends. Last weekend we saw Brutus the Barber Beefcake on WWF, and we copied his move for a show for the kids in the hall. The hair I threw in the air was from my dog, not Paul. We weren't fighting. You have to believe us!" He just shook his head and told us to go back to class. I'm pretty sure he couldn't wait to go home and tell his wife about us.

My antics weren't limited to wrestling between classes. For some reason, my Spanish teacher, Señorita Karen, didn't think much of my kind of humor. (I suspect I somehow reminded her of her ex-husband.) I took it as a challenge to have fun in her class. She had recently caught me taking bets from other students on how many times we could get her to say a particular word that day. She confiscated my "betting chart" and reprimanded me. While she was out of the room for a few minutes, I wrote something on the whiteboard I thought was really funny—not obscene, but definitely inappropriate, in both Spanish and English. (Think what a young Michael Scott would write, and you'll get the idea.) Then I pulled down a retractable projector screen to cover it. She only noticed when the next class met and she pulled up the screen to reveal the sentence of the day . . . but it was my sentence! She knew who had written it, and she told her class, "José Anderson will be an alcoholic, a compulsive gambler, and divorced by the time he's twenty-five!" By the time the next class started, my writing on the whiteboard and her blistering prophecy had circulated all over the school. Everyone wanted to know if I was going to complain to my parents or the principal. No way! I didn't want any of them to know that I'd started it.

I've heard people comment about the positive impact of a teacher and say, "Wow, she really saw something in me!" This was one of those comments, but in reverse. I don't know why we didn't connect very well. Other teachers played along with my jokes, but not Señorita Karen. But the next day, she must have felt a tinge of guilt for calling me out like she did to her next class. When I walked in, she said, "Hola, José."

I answered, "Hola, Señorita Karen."

She gave a stoic look and asked, "Are we going to have a good day today?"

I replied, "Si, Señorita."

We stared at each other to see who would make the first move to bring up what I did or what she said the day before, but neither of us gave an inch. It was a true Mexican standoff . . . in Spanish class! I stayed out of trouble in her class the rest of the year, but I never reengaged and ultimately failed Spanish because, unfortunately, *el gato se comió mi tarea.*

I was a first-class knucklehead. Years later when I reflected on some of the common themes and recurring statements I'd received, I realized that my parents, teachers, coaches, Sunday school teachers, youth leaders, and everyone else who took time to notice me had told me, in some way, "Joe, you never know when to quit!" I pushed things a little too far or too many times. I loved excitement and drama, and I always tried to make things fun.

After some of those incidents, I started getting more serious about my relationship with the Lord. Instead of only living to make people laugh, I became more focused on leading people to Christ. I still liked to have fun and joke around, but I started leading a Bible study, speaking out about my faith, and living out my relationship with Jesus. I had an amazing youth group, with great friends who have gone on to do wonderful things in ministry and life. The church's legendary Senior Pastor Jerry Strandquist and Youth Pastor Brad Davis saw potential in me and always encouraged me to use my creative personality for God. My relationship with the Lord flourished. I was able to direct my energy into youth group activities, create and perform in skits, and come up with innovative ways to reach other kids with the gospel. In all of this, God was reinforcing my call to preach and be a pastor. My church involvement was everything to me, and there was no place I'd rather be.

I felt created and gifted to be a pastor. For some reason, people seem especially willing to tell me things they haven't told anyone else. I guess I'm a good listener, and God has given me a lot of empathy for people in pain. I'm also known for my smile. Some have wondered if it's genuine ... it is. I'm like Buddy the Elf: "I like smiling. Smiling's my favorite."

Sundays were a rapid-fire series of events: Sunday school, worship service, lunch with youth group friends, run home to change clothes then back at church again for choir practice, Sunday night service with time afterward for prayer at the altar, then out to eat with friends until late at night. I dreaded facing all the homework I hadn't done yet. Wednesdays at church would start right after school—heading out to help set up for the youth service, and I usually had something to do during the service. I was living in my sweet spot of serving the Lord with friends who felt the same way. I was on a fast track to the ministry. My friends called me "Preacher Joe," and I felt strongly called to follow God for the rest of my life.

After graduation, I lived off the money I received as gifts at graduation while working as a counselor at our denomination's camp, Lake Geneva Christian Center, in Alexandria, Minnesota. It was an amazing summer, but it didn't help me save money for college.

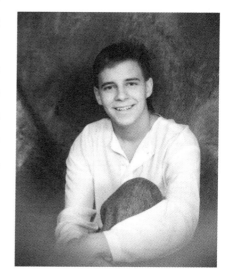

When I went to my first college classes, sadly, something changed. Like many other young people who were active in youth ministry before going to college, I drifted from the church and the Lord. My close friends scattered to other schools near and far—the band was breaking up! I wanted to go to North Central University, but I didn't have enough money saved, so I enrolled in a community college. I planned to work and save money while I got my general coursework out of the way. My new friends didn't have the same expectations of me, and as I heard their stories of partying and drinking, I wondered, *Have I been missing out on something?* I wasn't involved in the youth ministry at our church any longer, and I concluded that if I was ever going to "sow my wild oats," this was the time to do it. I assumed it would be just a short time of experimentation, a passing fad, and then I'd get back on track. I told myself, *Soon I'll be going to Bible college, I'll be a pastor, and I'll serve God for the rest of my life. What would it hurt to let loose for a little while at a place where no one is watching too closely?* Like the prodigal son, "the far country" started looking attractive to me.

At a fraternity party at the University of Minnesota in the fall of 1992, I got terribly drunk. I liked the full-body buzz, but my system couldn't handle that much that soon. I walked outside to vomit and ended up passing out in the yard. Later that night, I remember people walking by and poking me with a stick to see if I was dead. To their surprise (and relief, I hope), I popped up and, with a second wind and new life, I went back inside and started drinking again. My friends had been looking for me and were laughing about my quick recovery from being passed out . . . and that I immediately started drinking again. That's when my legendary drinking reputation began.

That was my introduction to alcohol. From the beginning, it did something in me and for me that was different from the effect it had on my friends. It clicked for me. I needed it to truly be myself. It made all my insecurities go away, and it made me feel really happy. I soon discovered that no matter how much I drank, I didn't get hangovers like my friends did. When I went to church after a Saturday night of drinking, I was relieved to discover that I wasn't going to be struck by lightning. The people at my church still saw me as the nice young man who was destined to be a pastor, the golden boy they wished their sons would become. Alcohol, I concluded, gave me tremendous benefits and no consequences—all good. No harm, no foul.

I'm not sure how it contributed to my obsession with alcohol, but I have a condition called synesthesia, so when I see numbers and letters, each one is a different color. I sort of see music in my mind's eye, and I feel things very deeply. I get a weird taste in my mouth in certain situations. It's like my senses get mixed up. I get embarrassed by how easily I get goosebumps. I'm *way* more sensitive than people think. It's not a disabling condition at all, but it feels like my senses are always set at 11 on a scale of 0 to 10. Other people have dimmer dials for their emotional lights, but I just have an on-or-off switch—for me it's usually all or nothing. I have to think this made me at least a little more susceptible to problem drinking. Like any other addiction, "One is too many and a thousand is never enough."

After a year of community college, I was miserable. I hated school, and I felt my life was falling apart. I was in the early grip of alcoholism and realized that I was living a compartmentalized life. I tried to act like a good Christian around my parents and the people who knew me back home, but I was living a lie. My close relationship with the Lord was a distant memory, but strangely, I still had a firm desire to follow the call to be a minister. That, I kept telling myself, was who I really was. But was it? What was going to happen to me? Which road would I choose? I kept telling myself I had to "get it together" while at the same time turning to the thing that kept tearing me apart.

In August of 1993, I decided I wasn't going back to the community college. I wanted to take a break from school and do something productive with my life. Ever since I was a little boy, I'd wanted to be in the military. In fact, I was infatuated with the military and idolized my grandfather and father because they had served. Like I said, my grandfather was a decorated WWII hero with two Purple Hearts. I was his only grandson, and he told me stories about the war and experiences that he had never told other people. My dad also served in the Army National Guard for about thirteen years, and some of his best stories revolved around the military. I remember as a kid being so excited when my dad would come home from deployments and training. I put on his uniform, and I felt so proud. Military service wasn't only something I wanted to do; I felt like it was my rite of passage passed down from my father and my father's father.

I joined the Air Force National Guard. It was a six-year commitment that included the same training as active duty and then one weekend a month during the year and a two-week deployment in the summer. Of course, our squadron could be activated at any time for war or local and national emergencies. My best friend Ryan had joined the previous year, so I joined him in the 133rd Security Forces Squadron (which is the Air Force Military Police). This would pay for almost all of my college expenses and give me a lot of other significant benefits. I was really excited and hopeful. I needed to take a break and change the trajectory of my life. It was an opportunity to reset for what was next—to reestablish my relationship with the Lord and prepare to be a pastor.

I left for six months of basic training and tech school for the Security Forces at Lackland Air Force Base in San Antonio, Texas, and Air Base Ground Defense in Fort Dix, New Jersey. I thrived. It fit like a glove. I loved the discipline, the accomplishment, the challenge, the history, the uniform, the medals, the spit and polish. I enjoyed the camaraderie with the other guys in our unit. Soon they saw me as a paragon of virtue, a fellow Airman

THE PASTORIZER | 39

destined to become a pastor. I enjoyed talking with them about the Lord, and amazingly, I kept my drinking a secret.

After my training was completed, I returned home for a few months before school started. For six months, I hadn't had a drink or used any chewing tobacco, but I started again. Addictions are confusing and cruel. When we're in the throes of it, we want nothing more than to be free, but when we aren't using, we long for the substance or behavior that puts us in bondage.

(Let me interject here that for those who aren't familiar with alcoholism, it's not like it's usually portrayed in movies and television shows. Not everyone is thoroughly wasted and completely out of control all day every day. Many hold good jobs and are "functional alcoholics." I was a binge drinker. I could do without alcohol for a week or two, and then go on a binge for a weekend. For those two weeks, I looked like any other normal person. This is why an alcoholic can go to jail for several years, and if not treated, they come out and pick up right where they left off. It's called being a "dry drunk." Alcohol doesn't need to be present for alcoholism to be a problem. Each time I binged, the urge became more intense. It's a progressive disease, gradually altering the mind and body so we can't function without it. We have to drink to feel "normal.")

I kept telling myself I'd quit—for good—before I went to Bible college because alcohol was forbidden for students and faculty. That would be the turning point; that would be the end of it.

In the fall of 1994, I transferred to North Central University as a sophomore. Jen was transferring as a sophomore from a school in Michigan. New students came to campus the week before classes started so they could get acclimated. One day during that week, I was on campus walking down a skyway (which, for you who live where it's relatively warm and seldom snows, is an elevated walkway so students don't have to go outside in the freezing cold), and I noticed three pretty girls walking toward me. One of them was amazingly beautiful—she looked exactly like what my dream girl would look like. Instantly, I thought, *I need to meet her before the rest of the upper-classmen arrive. I'll never have better odds to make a good impression!*

I stopped to introduce myself to the three of them, but I couldn't take my eyes off Jen—she was drop-dead gorgeous. A lot of my friends and I talked about the type of girl we preferred. Mine was the 1993 Demi Moore look. Jen was that, except even more beautiful. I told them my name, and then Jen said, "I'm Jennifer Peppard."

Immediately, I thought of the actor George Peppard, who played on *The A-Team*. The line his character was known for was, "I love it when a plan comes together." I asked her, "Are you related to George Peppard?"

She responded with a smile and said, "Yes, he's a distant relative."

I told her, "He's one of my favorite actors from the show."

Jen smiled again and said, "I love it when a plan comes together."

That sealed the deal. This girl is beautiful, she's funny, and she likes what I like. The clouds parted. I could hear the angels singing. I was ready to pick out an engagement ring right then!

I got her number, and we started dating soon after we met. But there was a problem: Jen is smart, witty, strong, and beautiful—a 10 out of 10 anywhere in the world, but I'm a Minnesota 6.4 on my best days. I had to make up the difference with my sense of humor and every ounce of charm I could muster. After we had dated for a while, I wanted to make our first kiss special, so I planned it carefully. When we were out together, I acted like I couldn't remember the name of a city in Florida: "I can't quite remember how to say it. Is it Kissy-may . . . or Kissy-mite?"

"No," she quickly said. "It's Kissimmee."

I grinned and told her, "Kiss me? I don't mind if I do!" And I kissed her. Corny? Absolutely. Worth it? You bet! (This may have been the only time in recorded history when this worked, so if you're a single guy and you're looking for an angle, don't even try it.)

We dated during the years we were in school together, but it was on and off. Even though I was head-over-heels for her, I struggled with

commitment. I'd break up with her, but I couldn't stand to live without her, so we'd get back together, and then I'd get anxious about commitment again. That happened twice. Each time we got close, I felt myself "falling for her," and it scared me. I loved the idea of her being my girlfriend, but I didn't like the idea of being committed long-term. It felt claustrophobic. Plus, I was doing the very thing I'd promised I would never do. Behind the scenes, I was struggling with drinking and chewing tobacco. I felt tremendous shame and guilt. Like the Apostle Paul described in his letter to the Romans, "For I do not understand what I am doing; for I am not practicing what I want to do, but I do the very thing I hate. . . . For the good that I want, I do not do, but I practice the very evil that I do not want" (Romans 7:15, 19).

I was living a double life. I was drinking (at a school that forbids alcohol) and hiding my addiction from everyone, especially Jen. In virtually every chapel service and a thousand other times, I prayed, "God, take this habit away from me!" I was hoping for a "holy zap" that would free me without any effort on my part, but it didn't happen. I was often very upset with God for not coming through like I hoped He would. I needed God to free me from alcohol! There was too much at stake to keep taking the risks: I was in Bible college to become a pastor, I was an intern in a great church, and I wanted to live with integrity. My girlfriend was all I could ever want in a soulmate. She's beautiful, loves Jesus, and is committed to go into the ministry. Everything was falling into place for a wonderful future—except for one very big piece of the puzzle. I'd become skilled in keeping the truth from people around me, and I was terrified that anyone would find out about my secret addiction. If I was found out, I was sure I'd be kicked out of school, my internship would be over, and I'd lose Jen. It's a terrible feeling to become addicted to something and not be able to stop it . . . to be too ashamed or prideful to know where to turn for help. It's a lonely and sad existence. Most people can't really understand it unless they've been there.

I remember one particular chapel service when I went to the altar. I knelt and raised my hands to beg God to free me from my addiction so I wouldn't have to lie and live in fear of being found out. I prayed, "Do it now, God!" I was hoping the fervency of my prayer would move God to answer me. But nothing happened.

I tried to cut deals with God. I promised to quit at the beginning of the next month, the next semester, or the next year . . . but not today, not now, not in the moment God had given me to repent. I kept kicking the can down the road. I wanted change on my terms so I could control people's opinions of me and I could avoid being exposed as a fraud. Much later I realized the problem wasn't God's care or His power—it was my lack of surrender. I had become skilled in compartmentalizing my drinking from the rest of my life. I told myself, *That's not who I really am. I can quit anytime.* For those who don't know, those are classic lies alcoholics believe.

Jen and I continued to date throughout that year, but my double life made me reluctant to make a commitment. Each time we broke up, I didn't give her a clear answer about why. This drove her crazy because our relationship was great and the breakup seemingly came out of nowhere. It was really a result of my internal struggles, my insecurity, and the fact that I was living a double life. I wanted to change, to be worthy of Jen, but I was well aware that if my secret got out, it would break her heart. I desperately wanted to change, but it wasn't happening. Each time, I told Jen that I just needed a break, or I needed to sort some things out about my future. I stopped short of the typical Bible college response of "God told me to."

After one of the breakups, I saw Jen in the lobby of church one Sunday. She motioned for me to come over, and she introduced me to her parents. In all our time dating, I'd never met them because they lived twelve hours away. I felt really awkward, especially when Jen's mother saw an opening. She looked at me and asked point-blank, "Why did you break up with my Jennifer?" JoAnne wasn't being malicious at all. She was just asking what she, her husband, and Jen were thinking. Jen gave a wry smile as if to say, "Yeah, Joe, why did you break up with me?" Her dad just started to belly laugh and looked away. I think he felt sorry for me. I had no idea what to say, which was exactly the reaction she hoped to get. I frantically and clumsily tried to change the subject, "The weather is beautiful, isn't it?"

It may be weird, but Jen's response that day made me love her even more. I saw that she's a tough cookie and I kind of liked the idea that she could put me in my place. I admired her strength.

It wasn't long before Jen and I got back together. We dated for the entire next year without any breakups. Her parents invited me to visit Jen and them in Michigan. That was a big step toward commitment. By the late fall of my senior year, I was convinced she was the one. I told my parents that I planned to ask Jen to marry me. They weren't surprised. Jen and I had Sunday lunch with them almost every week during the two years we'd been dating, and they liked her a lot.

The week before Thanksgiving, I called Jen's dad to ask for her hand. As soon as he realized what was happening, he asked, "Do you mind if I get JoAnne on the phone with us?"

I'd imagined this would be a man-to-man interaction, but I said, "Sure. That would be great."

Bill and JoAnne were very supportive, and they became comrades in my secret scheme to propose. Jen was home for a couple of weeks over Christmas, so we worked out a plan for me to fly to Detroit to surprise her on December 30th. Her mom was going to take her somewhere for the day while her dad picked me up from the airport and drove me to their house. When Jen got home, I'd be there for the romantic proposal. Bill and JoAnne were all in.

I was still a poor full-time student, but I wanted to get Jen the best ring I could afford. I went to the jeweler in Minneapolis. I picked one out and arranged to pay half at that point and the other half when I picked it up right before my trip to Detroit.

On a snowy Friday in Minneapolis, December 29th, I worked at the collection agency until almost five o'clock. It was the end of the month and the end of the year, so every minute matters when you're on commission. On the way to the jeweler, I had to fight through the triple threat of rush-hour traffic, heavy snow, and a busy Friday before New Year's. I got to the jeweler just before the store closed. I paid the remaining part of the bill and got the ring. By this time, I was already late for my scheduled six o'clock call with Jen. The weather was worse than usual, I got stuck in traffic, and I didn't make it home until seven. (Remember, this was before cellphones, so I had no way to call or text her to let her know I'd be late.) In those days, communication took a lot more effort and planning, and we had little room for error. Jen and I had to schedule appointments for phone calls, so being on time was a pretty big deal. She had been spending time with friends, and she had cut it short to be home for our call. When I finally called her, she was more than a little annoyed. It wasn't the most pleasant conversation. I couldn't tell her I was late because I was picking up her engagement ring, so I had no good excuse—at least, not one that made any difference to her. I hoped that she could hear it in my voice that I had *a very good* reason for being late, but she didn't pick up on my cues. Our talk was tense and short. I'm not sure she would admit that she hung up on me, but that's the way I took it. It wasn't the confirmation of love that I hoped we'd both enjoy during the call.

Early the next morning, I drove to the airport. After a layover in Chicago, I arrived in Detroit that afternoon. I didn't wear my usual Saturday casual clothes. I chose my outfit very carefully. I went with "smart business casual"—not too dressy, not too informal. I wanted to look like I knew what I was doing! I wore a thin maroon V-neck sweater with a white Oxford button-down shirt, my nicest khaki pants, and brown Doc Martin boots. It was a classic look. I was all set! I put the little box with the engagement ring in my front left pocket—over my heart and under the sweater. I was paranoid about losing it, so every minute or so I checked to be sure it was still there. I was also a little paranoid about what Jen's answer would be. The conversation the night before hadn't been the perfect lead-up to a sweet and glorious proposal! I was ninety-nine percent sure she'd say yes, but I began to wonder if she was having second thoughts.

On the flight from Chicago to Detroit, I sat next to a well-dressed lady. I kept putting my hand up to feel for the ring box in my top left pocket. Not long after takeoff, the lady reached over and put her hand on my arm. She said sweetly, "It'll be okay. I fly a lot. There's no reason to worry." She must have thought I was grabbing for my heart because I was afraid of flying. I told her, "No, no, no. It's not that. I'm not afraid to fly. Actually, I'm in the Air Force!" I told her I was going to ask my girlfriend to marry me, and I had the ring in my pocket. She was so excited for me. A number of people sitting around us overheard our interaction, and one of them asked the inevitable question, "Do you expect her to say 'yes'?"

I was shocked at the question. I wanted to ask, "Why wouldn't she?" But instead, I laughed and answered, "How could she say 'no'?" But the question made me wonder, *What if Jen actually said "No"? What would I do? Where would we go from there?* My mind raced in a bad direction: *I'll have to get a cab from the house back to the airport. I'll go to a pawn shop, sell the ring, and get a flight to Mexico for a week or two to hide so I don't have to answer awkward questions.* That would be terrible!

Bill picked me up at the airport. On the way to their house, I asked, "Do you think Jen suspects anything?"

Bill answered, "Oh no. She doesn't know a thing."

A few minutes later, I just had to ask, "Do you think she'll say 'yes'?"

I waited for his full-throated affirmation, but instead, with a smirk he said, "Yeah, I think she will."

Think so?

He dropped me off and left. Jen's mom took her out for the day. The plan unfolded perfectly: In the middle of the afternoon, JoAnne told Jen she'd forgotten something at home, and they needed to go back to get it.

As I waited, I lit a fire in the fireplace. I thought it would add to the romantic moment. I couldn't decide whether to be standing or sitting when she walked in. I'm not sure why it mattered, but it was one more thing to worry about getting just right. I hoped she'd come soon, but the minutes passed slowly. I had a good view of the long, winding driveway, and after what seemed like an eternity, I saw the car coming to the house.

When Jen's mom parked in their driveway, she asked Jen to go in and get the package. I saw Jen get out, and then she disappeared. She came in through the garage. The door to the house opened, and she entered like a woman on a mission. She looked a little miffed that her mother had forgotten something and they had to drive all the way back home to get it. (She looked beautiful, as always. She always looks like she's headed to a photo shoot.) Then she saw me sitting in a chair.

She exclaimed, "What are you doing here?"

She was smiling and laughing, so I took the question as a positive sign. She walked toward me with her arms reaching out for a hug, but before she got to me, I got down on one knee and held out the open box with the ring. I said, "Jen, I love you with all my heart, and I want to spend the rest of my life with you. Will you marry me?"

Jen was very surprised, and said, "Joe! Joe! Joe!" which to me, sounded too much like "No! No! No!"

I told her, "Hey, I'm looking for a 'yes'!"

She laughed and said, "Oh yes! Yes! Yes!"

We hugged and kissed. I put the ring on her finger and we prayed. We cherished the moment.

A little while later, Bill and JoAnne came home and joined the celebration. Then Jen's younger sisters got home from their temporary exile from the house, and they were almost as thrilled as we were. A few minutes later, Jen's older brother Greg and his wife Christa came. We had a lovely dinner together. It couldn't have been any better. Jen had been totally surprised, and her whole family shared in the magic of that day.

The next day was New Year's Eve. In the middle of the morning, the phone rang. JoAnne answered it and turned to me: "It's your mother."

I wondered why in the world my mother would call. When I picked up the phone, my mom didn't ask about the surprise or the engagement. Instead, she told me that the night before, when we were celebrating our engagement, one of my childhood best friends, Darryl Isaacs, had died in a car accident back in Minnesota. For me, he was one of those friends who makes you feel completely comfortable. We seemed to always be on the same wavelength. He was a good guy and loved the Lord. When I got off the phone, I sat down and wept. Jen put her arms around me to console me. Darryl was the first close friend I'd lost, and it hurt a lot. I felt sad and guilty. How could I celebrate when his family was grieving?

Our first day of anticipating our wedding suddenly had a dark cloud blow in. This was the first time in my relationship with Jen that something tragic happened right on the heels of something wonderful. It wouldn't be the last.

CHAPTER 3

THE HONEYMOON PHASE

And now, back to Milford . . .

Two weeks after the shooting, I loaded a U-Haul truck, and Jen and I headed for Minnesota—me eagerly and Jen very reluctantly. The weather was gloomy and raining, matching the mood inside the cab of the truck. During the entire trip, Jen leaned against the window and cried. She said she had a migraine, but I think it was PTSD and depression. The last two weeks had been a nightmare; our marriage wasn't off to a great start.

We unloaded at our apartment. After I returned the truck to the U-Haul dealer, I went back to our cluttered apartment. We'd planned to open our wedding gifts the morning after our wedding, but they were still wrapped when we put them in the truck. Now, with little joy, we opened the presents because we needed a lot of the gifts to cook and set up the apartment. I was grim and determined; Jen was withdrawn and silent. The first few days we just went through the motions, but every night, Jen talked to her mom and dad on the phone for one to three hours. It was apparent that she wanted to be close to them . . . but distant from me. And the long-distance bill was costing us a fortune. The cost shouldn't have mattered, but the fact that her conversations excluded me more and were costing us so much money added to the resentment that was building in me.

Jen was still in shock, and I was incredibly frustrated. I went back to the one thing that always brought relief, the one thing I'd promised myself I'd never do again. About once a week, I went out drinking. I made sure to come home after Jen was asleep, and I slept on the couch. Actually, it was easy to hide my drinking from her because she was so preoccupied with her father's health.

People who suffer from PTSD may seem numb for a while, but they can explode in anger. Intense feelings of emotional pain, abject terror, and rage lurk just beneath the surface, and it doesn't take much for them to find targets—like a detached husband or an unresponsive wife. Jen and I argued and fought about, well, anything and everything. We were on opposite ends of the spectrum in how we handle conflict. I felt so uncomfortable that I walked away, but she wanted to hash things out right then and there.

The trauma was still very real. When we'd left Milford just a few weeks earlier, a police officer told us to be alert and take precautions because our wedding must have had something to do with the shooter's motives. As you can imagine, we didn't sleep very well. Every sound in the night startled us. Could it be him? Bill had been shot when he was in bed. Were we next? We lived with constant hyper-vigilance and paranoia.

As Bill recovered from the gunshot wound and the surgeries while he and JoAnne lived in the safe house, a number of their friends advised them to move from Milford and change their names. They believed it was just too dangerous to stay there with the shooter on the loose. JoAnne was understandably fearful, but as she and Bill drove back to their home for the first time since the shooting, she had a moment of inspiration. She told Bill, "Yes, we can move, and we can change our names, but the devil will always know where we are. And more important, God knows where we are. He spared you, He gave us our home, and He called you to be the pastor of this church. We're not going to let the enemy win!"

Bill had felt the same way, but he had been very concerned about JoAnne. When she showed such courage, both of them became committed to stay in Milford and trust God for safety and effective ministry. He told her, "We're going to live in our house, we're going to love people without being suspicious of every new person we meet, and we're going to reach people for Jesus. I should be dead, but I'm not. God spared me for a reason, and you're right: we're not going to let the enemy win!"

During the weeks Bill and JoAnne were away from their house, people in the church cleaned up the bedroom, the stairs, and replaced the carpet. They repaired the hole in the wall, bought a new mattress for them, and installed an advanced security system. For the first few nights at home, Bill and JoAnne slept in the living room, but again, JoAnne found the inner strength to say, "I'm going back to our bedroom tonight." And of course, Bill went with her.

Jen and I got married in October, and we planned to go back to Michigan for Christmas. I knew it was the right thing to do, but I dreaded going back into that tsunami of fear and pain that I was sure hadn't dissipated very much since the shooting. Jen wanted to go to Milford as early and stay as long as possible, but I had to juggle my responsibilities at the collection agency and the church. She got really upset when I said we couldn't leave early enough. I had to work on Christmas Eve until 2:00 in the afternoon, and then we could start the twelve-hour drive in my 1987 Chevy Beretta to Jen's parents' home. Of course, it was snowing. We drove through Chicago and kept going on I-94 East. On the highway in Gary, Indiana, the car broke down. It was the worst possible place. Nobody wants to break down there. (No offense, Gary!) It was an industrial area without an exit anywhere near us. Cars zipped by, the car wouldn't start, and Jen was crying. We felt like the world was ending and we were stranded with no way to find help. We'd just purchased an early model flip-phone. I dialed 9-1-1, but cell service wasn't what it is today, so I couldn't get through. I was really frustrated, and Jen was crying her eyes out. In our moment of hopelessness, a guy driving a flatbed tow truck pulled in front of us. He got out and walked back to us. We didn't know if he was friend or foe. When he got close enough, he said, "Hey, it's dangerous out here. I can't let you stay stranded on the side of the road so late on Christmas Eve. I think there's a motel up the road. I'll tow you there." When we got to the motel parking lot, I tried to pay him for helping us, but he shook his head and told me, "No problem. Just consider it a Christmas miracle." I'm not sure I've ever actually met an angel, but if I have, it was this guy. He was wearing white coveralls, he was so kind, and he came to our rescue when we really needed help.

When we checked into our room, we realized it was probably a pay-by-the-hour establishment. It was nasty. Jen called her sister Jodi and her boyfriend, and they started the drive from Michigan to pick us up. Jen and I just sat in chairs until they arrived because the bed looked way too iffy. We got to Milford early on Christmas morning.

As soon as we arrived in Milford, Jen's demeanor was transformed. She had been anxious and upset since the shooting, but when we walked in the door of her parents' house, she was filled with childlike joy. I was sad that I couldn't make her that happy, and I was jealous and angry that she wasn't nearly as excited about me. While we were there, the investigators wanted to ask us a few more questions. They obviously weren't any closer to catching the shooter, but they wanted to follow every lead.

Jen was consumed with her mom and dad—it was like I didn't exist . . . until a moment when I wished I didn't exist. I was secretly using chewing tobacco behind her back, and I hid a can by rolling it up in a Vikings sweatshirt. (Skol Vikings! Or should I say Skoal Vikings? Sorry . . . I couldn't resist.) One night when the family planned to play some games, Jen was a little chilly. She went into our room and came out wearing my sweatshirt. My stomach dropped. Why did she have to pick up that sweatshirt? She was hurt, angry, and disappointed. It made the time with her parents even more icy between us for the next few days. And it created even more distance between us. I felt like the biggest jerk. I'd lied to her and got caught, so the next day when I mentioned that we needed to leave so I could get back to work, she was furious. To add insult to injury, the repair bill for my car was over $1,000. That was a rip-off and a fortune to me.

Back in Minneapolis, I felt a lot of pressure to appear to have things under control. I was doing well as a bill collector, I was finishing Bible college, and I had an internship at the church. At this time, I was also named by the Air Force as "Airman of the Year" for the state of Minnesota. It was the biggest honor I'd ever received. After that, I was viewed as "the golden boy" and "super trooper," and celebrated by generals and other high-ranking officials. On the outside, I was living the dream, but on the inside, I was a disaster.

When Jen and I attended church services, I wanted to present a happily married couple who were handling major adversity with strength and grace. We had to look like we were strong and full of faith, because if we looked weak, I'd never get a job in a church. It was all a lie.

That April, Jen's parents flew to Minnesota to be there when I received my credentials as a pastor. While they were there, they joined Jen in trying to get us to move back to Milford. To be fair, Jen was getting some pressure from her parents, but it was her desire, too. They told me they really believed God wanted us to move back. Bill offered to bring me on the staff at his church, but I knew it wasn't a good place for Jen and me. Bill and JoAnne were still suffering from PTSD, and they wanted their little girl near them. I already felt like an unnecessary appendage when I was with all of them, and going back would just make it worse. I wasn't giving an inch on the hopes of Jen and her parents, and Jen wasn't giving an inch to stay in Minnesota and be my wife. When I said, "No, we're not moving to Milford," they were all very disappointed. Jen interpreted every small problem or setback in Minnesota as a calamity, which psychologists call "catastrophizing." We were both in pain, and as the saying goes, "Hurt people hurt people."

Six months into our marriage, in May 1997, the Air Force National Guard conducted a weekend of training. I looked forward to being with men I respected, and even more, I really looked forward to getting away from Jen. These guys believed I was too good to be true—a young, strong Christian on a path to becoming a pastor who had no problem with temptation and sin. In fact, I'd gotten my credentials as a minister just a few weeks earlier. They had no idea that I was a closet alcoholic. But that weekend, I went out drinking with them. They were laughing that "We finally got the preacher drunk!"

That night, they invited me to go with them to a strip club, and I went along. The next morning, I woke up in our open barracks, and the first person I saw was a guy I'd led to the Lord months before. He stared at me with a look that said, "I can't believe you did that. You hypocrite." He was exactly right. A huge wave of shame crashed over me. My gaze drifted to another guy. The day before, I'd prayed with him for his mother who was very sick with cancer. Another wave hit me. I was such a fraud. I'd known it for a long time, but now the guys knew it too.

On the drive back to the Twin Cities, I don't think I said a word. When I walked into our apartment, Jen noticed a round container in one of my pockets. She demanded that I give it to her. It was a can of chewing tobacco. She'd caught me again in a lie, and she knew she had me. She grilled me about the weekend, and I erupted: "Okay, okay. Yeah, I went drinking with the guys." I was angry enough to tell her the whole truth: "And we went to a strip club."

She slapped me. With a mixture of tears and anger, she told me, "I'm done!" Only seconds later, she announced, "I'm going back home." I wasn't surprised in the least, and to be honest, I felt relieved that she was leaving.

I had failed Jen, I'd failed myself, I'd failed my parents, I'd failed Pastor Rob, I'd failed the guys in my squadron, and I'd failed God. For years, a particular verse had taken root in my heart: "You may be sure that your sin will find you out" (Numbers 32:23). My greatest fear was being exposed as a fraud. I'd been able to avoid this judgment day for a long time, but it had finally arrived. The waves of shame were punctuated with blame, and it felt good to point the finger at Jen. I could finally tell people how horribly she had treated me. She had been perpetually in a sour mood. In fact, she was depressed—helpless, hopeless, lifeless. She didn't want to do anything that would reconnect our hearts, and her rejection and apathy really hurt. I explained that she had sabotaged our marriage because she wanted to go back to live with her parents in Michigan—and it had turned out just like she planned! That was my story, and I quickly became skilled in delivering it.

A huge part in the problem was my self-pity. I painted myself as the victim—of Jen and of God. Jen had made a covenant with me, hadn't she? How could she be more dedicated to her parents than to me? Every moment of every day, the tension between us got a little more intense. Before long, I couldn't find anything good about her. Every decision was a friction point. She didn't like any of my ideas, and to be honest, I retaliated by arguing with her at every turn. One of the arguments I vividly remember was the day she asked me to send my résumé to her father so he could share it with other pastors near Milford. Jen thought this was entirely good and reasonable, but I saw her insistence as a betrayal of her commitment to me. When I didn't respond, Bill put more pressure on Jen to get it from me. When she pressed me, I got really angry. Resentment poisons the mind and heart. I wanted to shake my fist at God and accuse Him, "Why did You let the shooting happen on my wedding night? I made a commitment to You that that day would be the turning point, but You let me down!" It was one of the lowest days of my life. I didn't see any hope for the future. For the first time, but not the last, suicide looked pretty attractive.

I wasn't as helpless and hopeless as I felt. To be honest, all of these powerful, painful emotions were mixed with a sense of relief. I didn't have to lie to Jen anymore, and I didn't have to put up with her constant displeasure. I wanted a way out, and I thought I'd found one. About a week before the weekend with the National Guard, I had to file some paperwork about our wedding, and when I looked at the marriage certificate, I noticed that my birthdate wasn't right. It said November 27th instead of the 29th. I wondered, *Is this a loophole that would let me have our marriage annulled?* For six months, the storybook love connection and marriage had been nothing but a nightmare. But no, a simple clerical mistake wasn't grounds for annulment.

I finally realized the cat was out of the bag. I couldn't hide any longer—everything in my life had fallen apart. My identity had been wrapped up in becoming a pastor, a pastor married to a beautiful girl, and together we were going to be admired by everybody. My parents had been so proud of me, and people at the church had high hopes for me. Jen's parents had believed the image I'd presented to them, and they were going to be devastated (though they probably had heard enough from Jen that things between us weren't exactly ecstatic). Now it was all dust and ashes. I had let everyone down. I was exposed as a loser . . . as a liar.

My internship was at River Valley Church, so the first person I called was Pastor Rob Ketterling. I met with him in person to tell him what had happened. Then I drove the fifteen minutes to my parents' house to give them the bad news and stay there until Jen left. They were out of town, but my sister was there. She's only a year older than me, so we were very close as we grew up. I used her as a practice run to tell my story. It was one of the most heartfelt moments I've had with her. I shared the details of my life that I'd been hiding for so long. I was devastated. She was heartbroken but very supportive. Late that night, I went to her bedroom with a pillow and blanket like a little boy who had a nightmare and needed his big sister. I slept on the floor next to her bed and cried myself to sleep while she prayed for me.

My parents got back later that next day, so to kill time, I cut the grass and continued to rehearse what I wanted to tell them. I met them in the driveway and told them, "Hey, let's go in and sit down. There's something I need to tell you."

I framed Jen's leaving as "not really my fault." I told them how the shooting had traumatized her, how badly she had treated me, and that I'd tried everything to hold the marriage together. I explained that I'd been drinking, but I told them it was the way I'd tried to cope with Jen's strange blend of hostility and apathy. Again, not my fault. I hoped they'd believe me and not hear a word about "the other side of the story." They were surprised, but not shocked. They knew all about the trauma of the shooting, and they'd seen Jen's depression and withdrawal. They hoped it wasn't as bad as they feared, but we hadn't spent much time with them since we moved back six months before, so they didn't have a grasp of the severity of our problems. I told them the plan was to separate for a couple of weeks and then get back together to make it work. They saw me as the victim, just as I intended. I stayed with my parents until Jen's flight to Michigan later in the week.

When I met with Pastor Rob to give him my side of the story, he assured me that he would provide resources to help me take steps on the long road back. He took notes so he could explain the situation accurately (or accurately, according to what I was telling him) to the staff team, the board, and the district executives. He was very kind and supportive, but he let me know that this event could put credentials at risk. That week, Jen and I met with Pastor Rob a couple of times. He hoped the rift between us wasn't as drastic as I'd described, and maybe, just maybe, he could help us begin the process of restoration.

The denomination's District Superintendent, Clarence St. John, offered every assistance for my drinking and for our marriage. Pastor Clarence had been my mentor, like a dear uncle to me. I grew up with his sons and spent a ton of time at his house throughout high school. As I told him the story, his eyes filled with tears. He hugged me for a long time and told me he loved me. He promised to do anything and everything to help us, but I resisted every act of kindness. Maybe I thought I didn't deserve it . . . which doesn't square at all with self-pity, which claims I deserve much better than I'd gotten . . . but confused and convoluted thinking is common for people in situations like mine.

As word spread, a number of well-meaning people tried to give me advice. One of them told me, "I give my wife flowers, and she really likes that. Why don't you buy Jen a bunch of pretty flowers? I'm sure that'll help." Another guy instantly swung into problem-solving mode. He sees everything through a financial lens, so he advised me, "Joe, you need to take a long look at your income, debt, and expenses. Money problems are often at the root of relational difficulties." Someone heard about the arguments Jen and I often had and suggested, "If you don't argue, your relationship will be a lot better." Someone else told me, "Just think about happier times together, like when you were on your honeymoon." I had to remind him that our honeymoon was spent in the hospital waiting room hoping we wouldn't get murdered in our sleep. Not too comforting a memory. I'm sure those people were trying to help, but they had no idea what was really going on between Jen and me . . . and I wasn't about to confide in anyone who offered a simple solution to a very complex set of problems. I minimized my struggle with alcohol. I told people that I'd been drinking just a couple of times to relieve the stress, and one of those times, I did something really stupid. I always ended by saying, "And I'll never drink again."

Pastor Clarence pleaded with me to go with Jen to counseling before she went back to Michigan, and I finally relented. He assured me that the therapist was one of the very best, and God had used him to restore a number of strained and broken relationships. I had nothing to lose, and Jen agreed to give it a try.

As Jen and I drove the forty-five minutes to the counseling center, the atmosphere inside the car was icy. When we arrived we were told the therapist Pastor Clarence had recommended had to leave for a family emergency, and we were referred to another counselor in the practice who was putting in his hours to earn his license. When we walked into the room, I was apprehensive that anyone could fix our marriage, but I sure wanted it to happen. This was a Hail Mary desperation pass at the end of a game if there ever was one. We checked in with the receptionist and sat in the waiting room. Soon, the counselor came to the door and welcomed us into his office. I had expected a young guy who was just out of graduate school, but he was an older man with a bushy gray beard. My heightened senses gave me a bad vibe about this guy. I quickly concluded that he had probably been a counseling client for many years and decided to give the profession a shot.

As soon as we sat down, things got even weirder: He took a crucifix down from the wall and put it on the table in front of us. He said, "Will you ask Jesus to be present with us as we talk?" We nodded, and then he told us, "Let's hold hands and pray. I want each of you to hold Jesus' hands." Jen and I slowly reached down to hold the hands of a wooden eight-inch Jesus on the cross. I was thinking, *Are we being punked right now? I'm not sure you're supposed to even be doing this.* And here's the thing: I'm not trying to be crass or disrespectful, but it's nearly impossible to hold hands with somebody who is nailed to a cross. I had to take my pointer finger and thumb to kind of pinch where His hand was. It was soooo awkward. The counselor prayed and then launched into a long story about people named Mary and Ted: Mary had cheated on Ted, and Ted had a gambling problem. It sounded like he was using their story as an example for us. Finally, after a long description of their problems, I realized the counselor had been looking at the wrong file, and he had us mixed up with his next appointment.

I waved my hand and told him, "Hey, we're not Mary and Ted. We're Jen and Joe."

He looked stunned and flustered. He apologized several times. It was obvious that he wasn't prepared for us, so we got up and walked out. We passed by a couple in the waiting room and nodded to them. I was sure it was Mary and Ted.

If someone had taken a video of our interactions with the counselor, people would have had a big laugh. It's funny now, but it certainly wasn't funny then. Jen had a flight to Michigan the next day. Meeting with a counselor had been a huge step, our last resort to begin to mend our battered marriage, and the counselor had been confused about who we were. In my wildest dreams, I can't imagine it going any worse. What a clown show! It seemed like a confirmation that our marriage was doomed. We had a few moments of gallows humor on the way back to the apartment. Both of us said something like, "I guess it doesn't get any worse than that!" There was an unspoken sense between us that we'd been cursed. It was over. I took Jen to the apartment, and I went back to my parents' house. That night when I talked to Pastor Clarence and Pastor Rob on the phone, I could feel their sadness and disappointment. I felt bad that they felt bad.

The next day, I drove Jen to the airport. When we got to departures, I got out to help her with her luggage. The fact that we were getting a divorce didn't stop me from being a gentleman. I put her bags on the sidewalk, and then . . . I didn't know what to do. What's the protocol for dropping your wife at the airport when you're separated? A hug? A kiss? A handshake? A prayer? I just said, "Well, have a nice flight. I'll talk to you later." She grabbed the handle of her suitcase and walked away.

Jen and I had no plans to reconnect—it all felt so nebulous, so open-ended, so hopeless. Pastor Rob tried to give us some parameters: "Don't let this go beyond two weeks." But Jen didn't seem to have any desire to come back . . . ever.

I moved back into the apartment that day. Even after all the exposure and drama of the previous week, I felt relieved that I didn't have to play games and manipulate the truth, and I didn't have to be around the woman who had made my life miserable for the past six months.

The relief didn't last long. When you put an alcoholic in an apartment by himself, the results are predictable. I went to the liquor store and bought several bottles of bourbon, vodka, whisky, rum, tequila, and all the usual hard drinks, and a few cases of beer. Jim Beam and Diet Coke was my drink of choice, but I never turned down anything with alcohol in it. Sometimes I drank up to twenty beers a night, knocking back glasses of liquor between six-packs. Someone who heard my story asked why I wasn't taking drugs. The answer is simple: the military drug-tests frequently, and I didn't want to do anything to jeopardize my Air Force career.

I had a meeting with Pastor Clarence. He had to tell me that I was losing my credentials. I'll never forget his love and compassion. With tears in his eyes, he said, "Joe, I care way more about your soul than if you're a pastor or not . . . and Jesus feels the same way. We both want you to know you're loved and there's nothing too big for God to change or forgive."

My internship was over, and my wife had left me. I threw myself into my work at the collections agency, and I drank late into the night. I got up the next day and did it all over again. That's the definition of insanity: Doing the same thing over and over and expecting a different result. It was a miserable existence, but it seemed like the only game in town.

From time to time, well-meaning people would hear the story about Jen and me and comment, "You just need to go back to how things were when you first got married." They had no idea that all this started only hours after we said, "I do." When we told them that part of the story, they were surprised. They realized their solution might work for other couples, but not for us. I blamed God for everything—my drinking, the shooting, Jen's complete devotion to her dad, my dumb decision to go to the strip club, the counselor's goof up, and all of the pain and shame I was experiencing. But it wasn't over. Not even close.

A few months after the separation, my best female friend since junior high, Kristie, and her fiancé Jeff, told me they wanted to look at an apartment in our complex. In their application, they used me as a referral. On the day they came to look at an apartment, the manager told them, "Why don't I show you Joe's apartment?" When she opened the door, all three of them were surprised. Whisky bottles and beer cans were strewn all over the floor and the furniture. Plants that had been cared for when Jen was there had dried up and died. The kitchen was a disaster area. The apartment looked like a couple hadn't gotten along, the wife had left, and the alcoholic husband had trashed the place. It looked like that because that was the actual fact. When I got home that afternoon, a letter from the manager was taped to my door. It read, "I brought the couple, Jeff and Kristie, who used you as a reference, to see your apartment today. I'm very disappointed in its condition. We expect our tenants to keep their apartments at a much higher standard of cleanliness." I was furious with my apartment manager for showing my apartment without giving me a heads-up, and I was utterly humiliated. I was beyond embarrassed, so I called Kristie to apologize. She is a very caring and compassionate friend, so she tried to soften my embarrassment. She told me, "Joe, you should see how messy my dorm room can get!"

She tried to make it sound like it was no big deal, but I knew I was exposed . . . in front of someone I cared about. I said, "Kristie, I appreciate you saying that, but let's be serious. Your dorm room never looked like that."

I could hear the sadness in her voice when she said, "Oh, Joey, I'm so sorry you're going through this."

When my lease was up and I moved out of the apartment I'd rented for Jen and me, I moved in with three guys—two of my friends in the military and one who was a coworker. I was a ton of fun to be around . . . at first. For the first half of the night, I was the star of the party, but by the end, I was a disaster. This wore on them. Living with an alcoholic is tough even when you're a hard drinker. I guess I exceeded their intake because after a few months, they held an intervention to confront me about my alcoholism. This wasn't a classic intervention like you can see on the Emmy-winning series on A&E. These guys had drinks in their hands when they told me I was drinking way too much and needed to cut back. One of them spoke for all three: "Joe, we like to drink, but you take it to another level. We haven't told you this, but we take turns every morning to go into your room to check on you because we're convinced that one of these days you're going to be dead." It was a silly scene. They were trying hard to sound sincere, but their message was, "C'mon man, we care about you. Just drink like we do, and don't take it so far."

At that moment, I had to pick among three choices: drink myself to death, kill myself, or get help. During this time, I began to feel more and more hopeless. It's such a terrible feeling to not be able to quit something. A good definition of addiction is when a behavior (drinking, gambling, porn, eating, not eating, etc.) stops being a choice. Honestly, killing myself seemed like the best option. I woke up every morning with the thought that I could stop the pain by ending it all. One of my roommates had a shotgun in his closet, and every morning I had to fight the urge to pick it up and blow my brains out. I made sure I never went into his room.

When I watched other people drink, I was amazed. They could drink at a party and then not again until the next weekend. I wondered, *Why can't I drink like them? They can stop. What is it about me that I can't? Why is drinking ruining my life, but to them, it's pure fun?* I prayed over and over and over again for God to take the addiction away, but either my problem was too big for Him . . . or He didn't care.

A number of the others in our collections agency drank a lot. By that point, everyone I knew drank quite heavily, and I more than any of them. I made promises every morning that I'd taken my last drink and things were going to be different, but if I was fooling anybody, it was me.

During this time, I had cut off connections with all my Christian friends. I seldom went to church, but on those rare occasions when I attended, I always sat in the back. Each time during the service, I had an overwhelming sense of God's presence and love. And each time, I got up and walked out as fast as I could. I know those two sentences don't make sense when they're put together, but they made perfect sense to me. The reason? I didn't want to surrender. I didn't want to experience grace, the kind of compassion that God loves to give but I so obviously didn't deserve. I was filled with shame and fear . . . two feelings that aren't from God.

Coworkers at the collections agency told me, "Just get a divorce and start fresh." Some of Jen's friends gave her the same advice. I'm not sure about Jen, but I just didn't have the emotional and mental bandwidth to go through the grind of a divorce. And then there's the added shame of not being able to make a marriage—between two committed Christians—work. And anytime I thought about getting a divorce, I just got drunk instead.

Shame became my identity: I was a failure, a loser, a person who couldn't be trusted. As I was growing up, I heard adults say that the worst thing in the world is a fallen minister. When I was a teenager, I became aware of several pastors and youth camp speakers who committed sins that disqualified them from the ministry. When adults talked about them, there was a sense that these people had let God down, let their families down, and let the church down. Now I was one of them.

I had to find some diversions to have some semblance of sanity, and the Minnesota Vikings did the trick. The collapse of our marriage and my self-destructive addiction happened as the 1998 season was beginning, the season when the Vikings went 15 and 1, setting all kinds of records. I absolutely loved the team, and I was sure they were going all the way. My best friend Ryan and I had season tickets together, and as the winning streak continued, we planned to travel to the Super Bowl in Miami. Nothing was going to stop us! The Vikings seemed unbeatable, but in the NFC (National Football Conference) Championship, they lost to the Atlanta Falcons on a missed field goal by our star kicker, Gary Anderson. He had a record-setting season and hadn't missed a field goal or an extra point all year. The Vikings were easily the best team in the league that year, and Anderson was the best kicker. But this time, he missed a thirty-nine yard attempt, wide left, that would have won the game, indoors, on our home field. We ended up losing in overtime. It was a mythic moment in the history of the Vikings. The dream was shattered. For me, the loss had a metaphysical significance; I spiraled into a deep depression.

In fact, I was so drunk and depressed that I didn't go to work for three days. At some point, I looked in the mirror and asked myself, *What happened to me?* My marriage was a failure, I couldn't stop drinking no matter how hard I tried, and now, my team blew their best chance in years at a Super Bowl. You may think an NFL team winning or losing shouldn't be a big deal, but if that's your perception, you haven't scanned the stands during a game. A lot of people live for their home team . . . and most of them probably aren't using their loyalty to distract from a life that's a catastrophic disaster. The season had become a distraction from my horrible life—actually, a kind of false idol that had captured my heart—and now it was all over in the most disappointing way.

CHAPTER 4

JESUS TURNED MY WINE INTO WATER

The Vikings' loss had a devastating impact on me. It accelerated my depression and hopelessness, which brought me to the brink. I didn't see how I could ever be more hopeless and depressed than I'd been before the game, but this was even worse.

(Some people talk about how a sports team affected their lives with a win in the World Series or the Super Bowl, like the New Orleans Saints winning it all a few years after a devastating hurricane, but the Vikings saved my life by a missed kick. They came so close to going to the Super Bowl that year, but whether they had won or lost the Super Bowl in Miami, I don't think I would have survived.)

Whenever I saw my mom and dad, I tried to avoid talking about Jen and the pain I was experiencing. I certainly didn't tell them about my drinking. My mother is such a dear, sweet person. One day, she didn't ask me any questions. Instead, she started crying and said, "I know this is a really hard time for you. You don't have to say anything, but your father and I are very concerned about you. We love you, and we hate to see you in pain. We're praying for you." I nodded, but I didn't say a word. She continued, "About a month ago, the Lord impressed me to fast every day at lunch and spend that time praying for you."

It broke my heart to see how much pain I was causing my mom. I told her, "Thank you. I appreciate it. I'm doing okay." At times when I realized how much I was running from God, the thought of my mom fasting and praying for me haunted me . . . in a good way. I couldn't escape her love. It meant more to me than you can imagine.

One of my coworkers in the collection agency was a woman named Christine. She and her husband had been involved in Alcoholics Anonymous for years. It may seem hard to believe, but at that point, I knew nothing about AA and recovery. The Twelve Steps were as unfamiliar as Hammurabi's Code. (See, you probably haven't heard of it either.) I knew Christine "went to meetings," whatever that meant, but I could see that she was infinitely more secure, optimistic, and healthy than I'd ever been. I started asking questions. At first I asked the kind of general questions people use to get to know someone. Gradually, I asked more pointed questions about what happens in the meetings. Christine wasn't fooled by my sudden interest in recovery. Since the day we met, she knew I was a raging alcoholic. To someone in recovery, my symptoms were like a flashing neon sign.

Christine told me how much she'd learned from "the Big Book." She described insights about secrets and deception, the power of denial, and the fact that some people, true alcoholics, couldn't quit on their own no matter how hard they tried. It was like my chest had been zippered open and she had exposed the depths of my darkened heart. I wanted to insist, to myself at least, that what she was saying didn't apply to me, but I knew better. I was desperate for help. I was at rock bottom . . . or so I thought. Our conversations over the course of several days convinced me that Christine was on to something.

I looked around my friend Ryan's house, and I decided to start over with a clean slate. I built a fire in the backyard and tossed everything related to alcohol into it. I realized I'd taken a bottle of whiskey from one of my roommates, and I wanted to make it good. I went to the liquor store to buy a replacement. I bought a bottle, but then I bought several more. When I got back to the house, I gave him the bottle, and then I got roaring drunk. (This is how insidious addiction can be. On the night I was trying with all my might to get clean and sober, I subconsciously set myself up for failure by going to the liquor store because of my "guilty conscience" about replacing a bottle I'd taken. That's why alcoholism is called cunning, baffling, and powerful. I had failed within hours of making my greatest attempt in my own strength.)

I passed out sitting by the fire, and I woke up the next morning as my roommate Chris was leaving for work. He was concerned that I was lying in the grass next to a smoldering fire. When I woke up he was half laughing—relieved that I was alive. He said, "Hey, Joe, don't you have to work today?" It was a terrible feeling to wake up smelling like smoke, wet from the morning dew, with ashes stuck to my skin . . . and a giant dip of Copenhagen dried up in my mouth from the night before. And I was still drunk.

I was also filled with regret. If this was the result of my first day of sobriety in my own strength, I was hopeless. I was convinced that I couldn't get sober on my own, and finally, every shred of denial was completely gone. I called Christine and told her I needed help. She said she'd gone to Hazelden Treatment Center to detox and start the process of recovery. I thought, *If it worked for her, maybe it'll work for me.* I made the call to talk to people in the admissions office. The person told me the cost was $30,000 for a month there. I didn't have the money and my insurance wouldn't cover it, but she explained that they have a fund for people who can't pay the full amount. It turned out that it cost me about $2,000 after the scholarship, and I needed to pay half of that right away to hold my place.

After I got off the phone, I called my mom and dad. I told them the story—the one I should have told them when Jen left me. They were upset with me. They were still confused about what had happened to Jen and me, and now that I was telling them I was an alcoholic, the house of cards fell flat. It was no longer exclusively (or primarily) Jen's fault. I was "one of those people." People didn't understand addiction and recovery. After all, there were testimonies about instantaneous, complete liberation from sin in churches all the time. My parents wondered why God hadn't or couldn't zap me and release me from the bondage to alcohol. They swapped one confusing story for a different one.

Even though I'd painted Jen as "the problem," she had been going to a counselor during the months we'd been separated, and she told me several times that she wanted us to get back together. I called her and "came clean" about how bad my addiction had become, without any idea how she'd respond. Would this be the last straw? Would it close the door on any hope of reconciliation? To my surprise and relief, she was incredibly gracious. I told her about Hazelden and Christine's experience, and I explained that I was having trouble finding even the $2,000 I had to pay. Jen sent me $1,000, no strings attached. I was stunned by her mercy and generosity. If there had been a perfect time for her to give up on me, it was then.

I was accepted at Hazelden, but I had to wait a few days for a bed to be available. I was instructed by the intake nurse over the phone, "Whatever you do, DON'T STOP DRINKING before you arrive here."

I was more than a little confused, so I asked her to repeat what she'd said: "Are you sure about that? You just told me to keep drinking before I get there."

She explained, "Alcohol is the most dangerous drug to detox from, and you could die if you tried to detox on your own. You need medical supervision for the first few days."

I still couldn't believe what I was hearing, so I asked another question: "So . . . is it alright if I'm drunk when I get dropped off?"

I was sure I could hear her smiling as she told me, "Yes, of course. After all, we're a treatment center."

"Done deal. Showing up drunk is something I do best!" I replied.

She laughed.

When I woke up on Saturday morning, April 17, 1999, I made breakfast and decided I might as well start drinking early because by that afternoon I was getting checked in and would start my new sober life. I was hopeful, but apprehensive.

My roommate planned to drive me the two hours to Hazelden, but it was the NFL draft day, so I waited until the Vikings made their first-round pick. I sipped on a twenty-ounce bottle of Diet Coke with Bacardi 151 mixed in—it's 75.5 percent alcohol. Bacardi 151 was the strongest legal liquor available at the time. It has since been discontinued due to its being a fire hazard. No sense messing around with flavor or the volume of liquid needed—let's get straight to the point! As soon as the Vikings selected Demetrius Underwood at the end of the first round, my roommate and I immediately left for the trip. (Ironically, Demetrius Underwood is considered to be one of the worst first-round picks in NFL history—which was fitting for my life at that point.)

When I walked through the front door of Hazelden, I found myself in an environment where I was being taught by people who knew me better than I knew myself. As I read and studied the steps, I realized the recovery principles are straight from the Bible! They point people to God, encourage them to humble themselves so they can have a genuine experience of repentance, assist in building a community of honesty and hope, and provide a path to make amends to those who have been hurt by our behavior. It doesn't get any more God-centered than that, though over the years AA has watered down their spiritual message and now talk about a "higher power."

I knew I would go through a medical detox, and I assumed that would fix me. I was open to anything they wanted to try on me . . . just make me better! I hoped it would be over quickly and easily. I soon realized that detox only cleared my mind so I could think rationally and process the concepts I was learning. I'd been impressed that a lot of famous people had been patients at Hazelden. My room had an acoustic guitar left as a gift by Eric Clapton from his time there. I knew that Chris Farley had been through there too. He was my all-time favorite comedian, but the fact that he had relapsed and died of an overdose only two years earlier was very sobering . . . literally. Those celebrities had been asked to humbly admit they were powerless over their substance of choice and submit to the same soul-exposing and heart-changing process.

The units at Hazelden are set up like fraternities, with about twenty men in each unit. Each unit has its own traditions and history to build camaraderie. The building was next to a beautiful lake, we ate in a cafeteria, and we heard devotionals every morning. While I was in the medical wing to detox, a psychologist came to assess my situation. She asked me to tell my story, and as I explained what had happened over the past year or so, she fought back tears and her voice cracked. She told me our wedding dates were the same, and before she left, she said, "Joe, I sure hope you'll receive the recovery you need." My story had touched her heart. Her sadness made me feel bad. I thought, *I'm so pitiful I even make the intake psychologist cry.*

After a few days it hit me: this was just like church camp . . . but unlike any I'd ever been to before. It actually discouraged me to see how much the program was like a church camp. I wondered, *How could it cost all this money and take all this time for me to just put my trust in God? That's what I've been running from!* (In recovery, people joke that a month of treatment is where you spend $30,000 to find out sobriety is a free gift from God.) But soon, I realized there was no earthly solution to fix my problem. Jesus is the only answer. I got on my knees and prayed, "Okay, God. I've run from You for a long time, and I've tried my best to run my life. It hasn't worked. Today, I'm totally surrendering to You. This program is pointing me to You, to trust You more deeply than ever, to invite You into the deepest part of my heart and change me. There's nothing good in me. I can't make life work on my own. Lord, there's no Plan B. No alternative. No other way I'm going to make it."

This was the first time in my life that I really, really experienced the unlimited depths of God's amazing grace. I thought I knew what it was before, but I'd always thought, deep in my heart, that God grades on a curve: good people get special treatment; bad people deserve judgment—and I'd always considered myself to be one of the good people. Now, I came face to face with the fact that I had nothing to offer God, nothing to twist His arm and get Him to love me. I finally realized I deeply deserved judgment, and this understanding opened the door to experience God's grace—His love, mercy, and compassion that I didn't deserve.

The prophet Isaiah didn't spare the people from the harsh truth about their condition. They claimed they were following God by obeying Him, but Isaiah knew better. He prayed,

> "All of us have become like one who is unclean,
>   and all our righteous acts are like filthy rags;
> we all shrivel up like a leaf,
>   and like the wind our sins sweep us away" (Isaiah 64:6).

Finally, I began to see the problem with "righteous acts" that are really meant to inflate our pride and impress people . . . which cause us to "shrivel up" spiritually and be swept away by temptation and sin. I'd lied about my alcoholism, and I'd lived a lie by always wearing a mask of a "righteous person," though my heart was far from God.

I couldn't make myself righteous in God's sight. Only Jesus could do that for me, and it would require the biggest swap in all of history. Paul put it this way: "God made [Jesus] who had no sin to be sin for us, so that in him we might become the righteousness of God" (2 Corinthians 5:21). On the cross, Jesus took all my sins—past, present, and future—and bore the judgment I deserved. In exchange, He has given me His righteousness, so that when the Father looks at me, He sees His forgiven, loved, accepted, adopted child. I can't earn this gift; I can only receive it . . . gladly, joyfully, and thankfully.

I had been self-sufficient and self-absorbed, and it had almost killed me. "Pride comes before a fall," and my fall had been disastrous. That day, God reminded me of two parallel verses in James: "God opposes the proud but shows favor to the humble," and "Humble yourselves before the Lord, and he will lift you up" (James 4:6, 10). These verses have meant the world to me. They remind me to stay humble and surrendered, and they reinforce the promise that Jesus is my victory and He will lift me up.

God used the twenty-eight days at Hazelden to change the direction of my life, but even more, to soften my stubborn heart so I was more in tune with Him. In the program, every day was a battle between denial and honesty, lies and truth, faking it and being genuine, despair and hope. One of the principles of recovery, one that is found throughout the Scriptures, is the necessity of being brutally honest with God, yourself, and other people. For years, I hadn't just deceived other people; I'd deceived myself. I'd told myself I could quit at any time, that it wasn't that bad, that everything was going to be fine, that nobody knew. . . and then that there was no hope at all. None of that was true.

During the month of treatment, I made some of the best friends a person could ever have. My roommates and I made a very odd group. One was an extremely successful, gay stockbroker who had inherited a lot of money. Another was a talented and driven black attorney from Boston who had a rags-to-riches story. I was the white, twenty-four-year-old fallen minister who needed a scholarship to be there. When we looked at our friendship, we said it was the perfect setup for a joke: "A gay stockbroker, a black attorney, and a white pastor walk into a bar . . ." I was amazed at their honesty and courage. We encouraged each other to take one more step, and then one more. When a person finally looks inside, it's like opening Pandora's box—all kinds of hidden hurts, fears, anger, and shame boil to the surface. It's ugly, but it's necessary. Recovery isn't an individual sport; it takes a team.

Alcohol doesn't play favorites. It can ruin anyone. In our unit, we had about twenty men who had arrived on different days so they left on different days when their twenty-eight days were over. New guys had "that look" of being stunned by the rush of reality, but as they worked the steps, they soon experienced real hope and healing. In addition to the two guys I mentioned, I spent time with a judge, three attorneys, a lot of younger guys with trust funds, and other people like me who were just trying to find a way to make life work. One of my closest (and most unlikely) friendships was with a famous New York attorney. The men from that part of the country had seen his commercials on television. He was one of the most interesting people I've ever met. For some reason, we clicked. He had to humble himself and make the same commitments we all were making. We were in it together.

One of the most misunderstood parts of recovery is about being anonymous. It's not just about keeping it a secret of who's there: *What you hear here, whom you see here, let it remain here when you leave here!* That's part of anonymity, but even more, it's the equality of your identities. Whether you're a doctor, judge, attorney, pastor, or teacher . . . unemployed, homeless, or wealthy . . . you're all equal as alcoholics. Addiction is the great equalizer—it's the same concept that we're all equal at the foot of the cross.

About half of us were under thirty, and the other half were sixty or older. We asked a counselor about this odd split, with very few in the middle, and he explained, "It's the difference between Type 1 and Type 2 alcoholism. In Type 1, people binge drink, and they suffer the consequences very soon. They quickly get to resolution one way or another: prison, a psych ward at the hospital, death, or recovery—in other words, the bottle, the big house, or the box. Type 2 is the slow-burning kind, a lifestyle of casual but regular drinking that seems under control . . . until it isn't. Denial is a much stronger obstacle for those people because they can point to a successful life—or one they've defined as successful. They come for treatment only when they experience significant health problems, or more often, strained and broken family relationships related to their drinking. Their adult children confront them and challenge their denial, and they don't want the grandchildren to be around them until they get sober. That's why the older group comes to us."

Some of the men had come to treatment only when their marriages or careers were destroyed by their drinking and drugging. Several of them advised me to file for a divorce. Their rationale was simple: My relationship with Jen had spurred more of my drinking, and I needed to avoid her if I was going to stay sober. I understood their logic, but as the weeks progressed, my mind became clearer and I was getting stronger. Now I had more hope that Jen and I could be reunited.

When I left Hazelden, I moved in with my parents. I didn't want to go back to the house with my three friends. It held too many bad memories. My roommates were supportive, but I didn't want them to have to walk on egg-shells around me or change their lifestyle because of me. This was my battle.

While I was in treatment, Pastor Rob started a Christian recovery pro-gram called Celebrate Recovery, and he led it. He wanted CR to be up and running by the time I got out. It was one of the most kind, thoughtful things anyone has ever done for me. In those first weeks, sometimes it was just Pastor Rob, another guy, and me . . . and sometimes it was just the two of us. He's incredibly busy, so I tried to convince him that he didn't need to lead the meeting, but he insisted, "No, Joe. This is important. I want to be here with you!" Before long, more people came, and Pastor Rob turned the meeting over to me and another recovering alcoholic. I went to AA multiple times a week and Celebrate Recovery on Tuesdays.

When I went back to work, Christine wanted to hear all about my time at Hazelden. I went to a few AA meetings with her and her husband. They were very supportive. God put her in that cubicle next to mine so she could give me the direction I desperately needed at just the right time. I'm sure of it. Interestingly, I was more productive at work than I'd ever been. I had thought I was at the top of my game all those years, but it was liberating to work without the dark cloud of addiction hanging over me.

Liberating, yes, but still hard. In those first weeks and months back, I was well aware that I needed to steer clear of certain people and places. I drove miles out of the way to keep from going near bars and liquor stores I'd frequented. In fact, when I saw a billboard advertising a certain liquor, I changed my route so I wouldn't have to see it again. When I saw an ad, a store, or a bar that made my mouth water, I spit it out. I didn't even want to swallow the saliva. I wanted to avoid even the hint of temptation. Some nights, I stared at the clock and counted down the minutes until the liquor stores were closing. When that moment passed, I could breathe a little eas-ier. I'd survived another day.

I posted a calendar in my cubicle to count the days I'd been sober. I thought, *I have to make it to ninety days.* I was meeting Pastor Rob at Celebrate Recovery, and I attended AA meetings. I was on the right road, but it still had plenty of potholes. I had to set up really strong boundaries because many people in the collection agency and the Air Force drank . . . and often drank a lot. I told people about my addiction and recovery so they wouldn't offer me a drink or make fun of me for not drinking.

The craving was still there, but it was fading . . . very, very gradually. I saw it as "a thorn in the flesh" to remind me of God's grace and power. I was desperately dependent on God. I knew that if I went back to drinking, I'd probably die from alcohol poisoning, a car crash, or suicide. It wasn't enough to "cut back" on my drinking. It was radioactive, a matter of life and death. I needed to be around people who understood this fact. My network of friends was changing. I no longer hung out with my drinking buddies, but I was building new relationships with people in the recovery community— people for whom I have the highest respect for their integrity and courage.

I was well aware that most people who go through recovery eventually relapse, maybe once, maybe many times. Later as I reflected on my experience, I came to the conclusion that if I'd gone into treatment earlier, I probably would have relapsed, and I may not have returned to sobriety. But if I'd waited any longer, I might have died one way or another. God had put me in the sweet spot—not too soon, not too late—another mark of His grace. I'm not an expert on this, but I suspect that when people relapse, it's because they still have a tiny shred of confidence that they're not in such bad shape and they can handle it. I had absolutely no confidence in my ability to control my drinking, and I think that's why I was so cautious about being exposed to people, situations, places, and ads that might tempt me to give in "just this once." In a sense, I'd relapsed a million times, promising myself every morning that last night's binge was the final one, but then giving in a few hours later after work. Relapse had been my way of life. I've never been under the illusion that I could drink again. I knew beyond a shadow of doubt that I couldn't, and if I did, it would kill me.

I had a close call one time when I let my guard down at a wedding of one of my friends. At the reception, the couple had an open bar. I asked the bartender to give me a nonalcoholic beer. She slid a real beer to me with a bit of a smile. Immediately, I felt panicked. I'm sure I looked like I was in shock. I stared at the bottle for a few seconds, and she asked, "Is something wrong?"

I suddenly realized even going to a bar to get a nonalcoholic beer was a really dumb thing to do. I was playing with fire. "Run, Forrest, run!" I turned and jogged away from the bar to the bathroom. I went to the sink, splashed water on my face, took some deep breaths, and prayed in the Spirit. The reception wasn't a good place for me at that moment, and I needed to get away. I said some quick goodbyes and left.

God was in the process of reengineering my environment. I had very different friends who talked about anything and everything except getting drunk, and my mind was clearer so I could make better decisions. One of the guys in Celebrate Recovery, Ron W, had been sober for ten years, and we became close friends. He was my accountability partner. Actually, I had a number of people who were accountability partners. I knew I could call on them day or night. My continued recovery was a blend of AA and CR—the structure of one and the Christ-centered nature of the other.

Jen and I continued to talk. She often expressed her desire to get back together, but I was afraid of messing things up again. Through her counselor in Michigan, Jen had resolved a lot of the trauma and fear around her dad's shooting. When they talked about her relationship with me, the counselor suspected that I might be an alcoholic or an addict. Then, when I entered recovery, Jen had renewed hope that the huge problems that had ripped us apart could be resolved, and our relationship could be mended. After my time at Hazelden, I held nothing back from Jen. In AA, Step 8 is, "Made a list of all persons we had harmed, and became willing to make amends to them all." Jen was at the top of my list, and my amends included being honest about all my deception and asking her to forgive me. She was amazingly kind and forgiving. It seemed that the only thing that could ruin our relationship was me, my drinking, and my lies. If these were resolved, then . . .

Jen was a flight attendant, so we talked when she was in cities all across the country. She really wanted to get back together. I talked with her about the possibility a number of times, but I always got cold feet because I feared commitment . . . and I feared a repeat of our past. It was a painful back-and-forth for Jen, with me backing away. Finally, she announced, "Joe, I'm moving back to Minnesota to see if we can work things out. I put in for a transfer from Detroit to Minneapolis." What? I was just getting my feet under me! Was she serious? Was I ready? It didn't matter—she was coming. Actually, if she hadn't taken the initiative, I don't think I would have ever budged. She had faith in God, she had confidence we could make it this time, and she had just the right amount of sass to push me in the right direction.

Things began to happen very quickly. Her transfer was finalized, and Jen was ready to come to Minneapolis. We needed a place to live, but I had no clue where it would be. Pastor Rob's grandfather had recently passed away, and his condo was empty. Pastor Rob invited Jen and me to move in and just pay the utilities. It was another amazing gift from Pastor Rob and his family.

Our two-week separation had lasted two years and ten months.

When people heard that Jen and I were moving in together, I thought they'd cheer, but it set off a firestorm. Suddenly we realized that all the anger and accusations we'd thrown around about each other when we split was coming home to roost. Our families and friends had taken sides—just as we hoped they would—and now they were just as angry, just as suspicious as they were in the weeks we'd asked them to believe our sides of the story. Her side had concluded that I was a raving maniac, and my side believed Jen was a monster. They told us we were crazy to get back together.

A lot of hurtful words were thrown at each of us. The pent-up resentment spewed out, and those words were hard to hear. Strangely, opposition only shoved Jen and me closer together. We defended each other, protected each other, and depended on each other. I would never have orchestrated our reconciliation this way, but God did.

To be fair to all those people, they hadn't seen a process they could count on. We hadn't gone to couples' counseling, and we hadn't given them a heads-up on all the conversations we'd had in the previous months. We'd left them in the dark. We certainly hadn't intentionally deceived them in any way, but it's understandable that they were surprised. (Even I was surprised!) They were being protective of us, and I appreciated their love and concern, even if it made our reunion with them pretty awkward at first.

On the day Jen and I moved into the condo, I felt like we needed to shake hands and introduce ourselves. A lot had happened since Jen's first day at college on that skyway, and we needed a fresh start. It was strange: so much time had passed that we didn't really know each other anymore. The calls over the months since I'd gotten sober had built a bridge between us, but it was made of rope, not steel and concrete. Still, it was a lot better than throwing firebombs at one another! We needed to get to know each other again. She was meeting her husband who was no longer living a lie, and I was meeting my wife who had suffered severe trauma. We stepped into the condo because we believed God had initially called us to get married, and He hadn't given up on us. We were obeying His voice. In our steps of surrender and obedience, God breathed life back into our marriage and rekindled our love.

Our transition from abandonment to face-to-face wasn't an immediate 24/7 matter. Jen was often flying for a couple of days at a time, and I worked a lot of hours at the collection agency. We spent enough time together, though, to remember why we fell in love in the first place. Sometimes I talk to people who are getting divorced, and they say horrible things about their spouse (or ex). I want to ask them, "You're saying those condemning things now, but wasn't there a time when you genuinely loved each other?" Jen and I were spending a lot of time remembering when we genuinely loved each other, and the feelings returned.

People mistakenly think that love and hate are opposite sides of a coin, when in reality, they're the same side. Love and apathy are the true opposites. When somebody really hates another person, it usually means at some point there was great love or expectation for love from them.

Forgiveness is unilateral, but reconciliation requires both parties. If only one of us had been willing to surrender to God's calling, it simply couldn't have worked, but thankfully, both of us were on board with His will. The furniture owned by Pastor Rob's grandfather had been taken out of the condo, so Jen and I had to make do. We had a fold-up card table for our dining area where we ate a diet of toasted bagel sandwiches, Cheez-Its, and Diet Cokes. We didn't own a television, so we spent our evenings listening to Christian radio, playing cards, and talking. We look back on that time as one of the best in our lives.

Right away, we went back to church at River Valley. On that first Sunday, Jen and I went forward to pray at the altar. We put ourselves and our marriage in God's hands. We trusted Him to heal the wounds of the past, and we depended on Him to lead us into the future. Plenty of people knew about our separation because I'd been so involved as a volunteer and an intern. Now when they saw us, they didn't know what to think. Sometimes, when people looked at us and then turned to say something to their friend

or spouse, we imagined they were talking about us and wondering how in the world we could live together again. Part of that may have been real, but I think we imagined a lot of it. Some of them had been close enough to us to take sides, and they needed us to convince them that those accusations had been way overblown, if not outright lies. Within a couple of months, their suspicions and doubts were resolved. People realized God was doing something special in our marriage, and they celebrated with us.

My parents and Jen's parents were thrilled that we were back together. They seemed to forget or overlook all the things that had driven us apart. We spent Thanksgiving in Michigan with her folks and Christmas with my family.

At our worst, we'd lived out Jesus' words, "Out of the abundance of the heart, the mouth speaks." The abundance of our hearts had been fear, rage, and shame, and that's what came out of us. Now we were living on the other side of that spiritual equation. In 1 John, it says that we love others to the extent that we've experienced God's unconditional and abundant love; Ephesians 4 says that we're able and willing to forgive those who hurt us only when our hearts are melted by Jesus' forgiveness of our sins; and Romans 15 says that we accept people who are different from us, who are outsiders, only when we're gripped with the truth that we were the ultimate outsiders but Jesus accepts us as His own. The love Jen and I were experiencing in our relationships was only because we were tapping into the true source of limitless love, forgiveness, and acceptance. Our hearts were filled with grace, and that's what was coming from our lips.

I've heard people say that in conflict, you need to go back and resolve every hurt and every painful word. If Jen and I had tried to do that, we'd still be dredging up terrible memories. You simply can't unscramble eggs. Yes, we need to be honest about what we've done and admit the hurt we've caused, but we don't have to pick apart every moment to confess them one by one. As we talked, Jen knew that I was deeply sorry for the pain I'd caused her, and I knew she was sorry about the anger and resentment she had directed at me. The same is true in our relationships with family and friends. We didn't need to dredge up every unkind word any of us had uttered. It would have only thrown more fuel on the fire of resentment. People know if we're sincere in our vulnerability, confession, and repentance. That's enough, and that's magnificent.

A counselor told me that bitterness is so attractive because it gives us two things we desperately want: identity and energy. We can claim we're the "one who was wronged," so resentment and self-pity make perfect sense. And protracted bitterness raises our adrenaline level, so we're "always on," ready to do battle with anyone who dares to disagree with us about anything. Bitterness can become so entrenched that it feels completely normal. In fact, we can't imagine living without it.

I thought about Jesus' encounter with the man at the pool of Bethesda. He'd been a cripple for thirty-eight long, grueling years. When Jesus saw him and discovered that he had been an invalid for so long, He turned to the man and asked a simple but profound question, "Do you want to get well?" (John 5:6) In any painful condition that produces bitterness and gives us identity and energy, this isn't an easy question to answer. In recent years, I've asked this question to people who struggle with addictions, food disorders, gambling problems, and years of heartache. To my surprise, many of them answer, "No, I don't want to get well." The familiarity and perceived benefits of staying sick outweigh the risks and unknowns of change.

It's a question Jesus asked me when I first thought about entering a recovery program, it's one Jesus asked Jen during the long season we were estranged, and it's one He's asking many of us today.

After Jen and I got back together, and about two years after I'd gone to Hazelden, I faced one of the biggest tests of my sobriety: that summer I went on my annual two-week training with the Air Force. I would be with some terrific people, but they loved to drink. I had to be ready. Before I left, I asked twenty-eight men from church to sign up to pray for me, two each day, in the morning or at night. I actually made laminated prayer cards for each specific period as a reminder. I explained, "I need to know people are praying for me and holding me accountable. I really appreciate you holding me up in prayer. And I'll pray for you at the same time." I kept a list of who had signed up for each slot.

While I was at the training, I looked at the list each morning and night. I pictured that person praying for me, and I thought, *I have to be strong for Leon, Brad, Chris, Rick* [or whoever it was at that hour]. *I don't want to let him down. Lord, give me strength to be true to You today!*

I told the airmen, "I've been sober for a while now, and it's been tough. I'm not going to drink with you anymore. That doesn't mean our friendship has ended. We might even become better friends now! I don't want anything to be weird. If you're drinking and I walk by, don't try to hide it. I'm fine with you being yourself. Please don't offer me a drink, but if I feel uncomfortable and get up and walk out, that's on me, not you." There wasn't anyone who thought I was overreacting. They were all very supportive because they'd seen my struggles firsthand and appreciated my commitment to change. I was open about my time at Hazelden and my recovery. In fact, I had some of the richest spiritual conversations with them during those two weeks. They wanted to know what happened to me, and I was glad to tell them about God's work to break me and build me back up. Those two weeks proved to be a major step in my recovery. It felt like a two-week missions trip because of all the opportunities I had with my guys. It taught me that the best defense is a strong offense—if I'm going into a difficult situation, go all-out with prayer and treat it like I'm on a mission with purpose. I'd been honest with drinking friends, I'd set boundaries without being offensive, I'd enlisted the prayer support and accountability of great guys, and I stayed sober. It was a huge win.

CHAPTER 5

"BABY, BABY, BABY, OH!" [1]

Within a few months of moving in together, Jen and I bought a townhouse and moved out of the condo. Things were looking up! Our love had been rekindled, and we focused on a hope-filled future instead of the distressing past. Jen enjoyed being a flight attendant, and I had gotten a promotion to management at the collection agency. We were experiencing the love we'd hoped to enjoy on the honeymoon we never had.

We were very involved in church, and it seemed all of the sideways looks from people who wanted to see if this new phase of our relationship was real had subsided . . . or maybe we were just too happy to notice. I was staying sober, and it wasn't as much of a challenge as it had been in those first months after treatment. I'd begun working on the process of getting my credentials as a minister back.

Pastor Tommy Orlando was the associate pastor at River Valley, and we had been close friends for years. As soon as Jen and I went back to the church, Tommy asked us to host a young couples' small group. I told him, "Thanks, but I don't think we're ready."

Tom tried to make it easy to say yes. "Another couple will lead the study. I just want you and Jen to host it on Friday nights."

Again, I told him, "Tommy, I don't know. I think it's too soon."

A few days later he called and said, "Joe, I signed you up. The group is meeting at your house next week. It's done. You'll love it."

Although I needed a kick in the pants to engage in ministry again, it was one of the best moves we could have made. The people in our group became some of our closest friends who supported us when we needed them most. I'm forever grateful for them.

In those long, terrible years Jen and I were apart, one topic that never surfaced was having children. Now, a year after we got back together, we were excited to start a family. After a few months, Jen felt nauseous one morning. She took an at-home pregnancy test, and we could hardly wait for it to register: we were going to have a baby!

We talked about names, we planned to buy a crib and a rocking chair, and we started looking at all the cute things that go in babies' rooms. We felt so blessed, so grateful. Could this really be happening to us?

We were so excited that we looked at a website every day to see what was happening to our baby. At twelve weeks, the site said that our baby was the size of a plum and was fully formed, but with lots of maturing to do. We were nesting and dreaming of what our baby would look like, and what personality he or she would have. We enjoyed every moment of it. We told the exciting news to everyone we knew! Jen took prenatal vitamins and did everything by the book. It was the first time she had given up caffeinated coffee since middle school. One evening, just past the twelve-week mark, she started bleeding. Panic overwhelmed both of us. Sadly, within a day, she lost our baby in the toilet. *In the toilet!* Not a dignified way to lose a baby.

Both of us wept until we didn't know if we had any tears left. For Jen, the physical pain was hard, but the emotional pain of losing the baby was worse. She told me, "I don't think I'll ever feel joy again." The miscarriage seemed so cruel, so unnecessary. There was no closure. Jen was angry, devastated, and confused. For weeks she cried out to the Lord and didn't hold back from expressing all of her powerful emotions. We didn't know why this had happened to us, but we chose to cling to the One who did.

The miscarriage was devastating—certainly because our dreams for our child were dashed, but even more because the trauma brought up all the old feelings we'd suffered after her father was shot. It seemed that whenever something wonderful happened—like our wedding or getting pregnant with this baby—a tragedy was just around the corner. Now we wondered again if we were cursed.

We prayed, we talked, and a lot of friends encouraged us. The fear and doubts gradually gave way to new hope, and we talked about trying again. A few months later, Jen got pregnant again. This time, we were more guarded about our dreams of what the future would be like for our little family, but ultimately, we fully embraced this pregnancy with all our heart. Once again, we tracked the growth of our little one growing in Jen's womb. We planned, dreamed, prayed, and told everyone our exciting news. This time Jen was reassured by hearing the heartbeat of our sweet baby. She shared in the joy of talking about a future baby shower with other friends who were also pregnant. But again at twelve weeks, Jen started bleeding and lost the baby. We were in disbelief and shock. How could this happen again? It was too much to bear. We were completely heartbroken. We never got to hold them, to cuddle them, to show them how much we loved them. Jen's grief was doubled over losing two babies, but once again, she chose to surrender her hurt, pain, and anger to Jesus. She still grieved, but she didn't grieve alone.

In the months Jen was pregnant with both babies, her identity shifted, and she began to see herself as a loving, protective mother. She believed that being a mom was a central part of her God-given calling. Her disappointment was doubled every time we spent time with other couples because many of them were pregnant, had little babies, or were having fun with their darling children. The heartache for both of us, but especially Jen, multiplied every time we were with our friends. Why them? Why not us? We weren't jealous. We were sad and confused. We were genuinely happy for our friends and family members who were having children, but we couldn't shake the question: Why can't we live a normal life with normal expectations and normal problems? Some of those friends tried to be very sensitive to us by not talking about their babies, which made us feel bad that they couldn't be themselves around us. It was all so awkward and sad.

On Mother's Day at the church, Pastor Rob asked all the mothers to stand so we could appreciate and applaud them. Jen just sat and sobbed. Our prayer wasn't complicated. We said, "God, we want children. We want to be great parents and raise our kids to know, love, and serve You." I added, "And Lord, I'm sober. I'll be a good dad. Please give us a chance to be parents that honor You." But as we expressed our hopes, it didn't take long for our prayer to change to: "God, look what happened on our wedding night. Don't You think You owe us? Why is it that teenagers can have sex and get pregnant when they don't want to, but we want to and can't carry a baby to term? It just doesn't add up. Please, just give us a baby!"

Jen and I had been separated almost three years, from June 1997 until April 2000. The next year had been tumultuous with the crushing disappointments of the miscarriages, but in the summer of 2001, we decided to try once again, as soon as I got home from deployment. My Air Force Security Forces squadron needed to send a team of twelve to support military operations for drug interdictions in Curaçao, a beautiful little island in the Caribbean. Our mission was to guard and protect the E-3 Sentry (AWACS) plane stationed there and the sensitive information being downloaded from the flights. We were gathering crucial intel on drug trafficking planes. We didn't know it at the time, but the drugs were funding a terrorist organization called Al-Qaeda. There was a lot of behind-the-scenes work to identity an evil organization that would soon become a household name.

Our squad was planning to return from deployment in the middle of September. I had been promised a promotion and a nice raise at the collection agency when I got back, but on the morning of September 11, everything changed. Terrorists commandeered commercial planes and flew them into the World Trade Center, the Pentagon, and a field in Pennsylvania.

We had to stay on the island until the air traffic chaos subsided, and we didn't know how long that would take. There were lots of rumors. One report said there may be terrorist cells on Curaçao, and we had to take every threat seriously. There were only twelve of us, and we were staying in a hotel. We set up an armory in one of the rooms. To blend in, we always wore Hawaiian shirts and shorts, and we carried our weapons discretely. The flight crew connected to the airplane left for urgent duty on the mainland, so we were on our own.

I was aware that as a flight attendant, Jen's flights that week had stops in Pennsylvania and New York, so when I heard the news that morning, I instantly tried to call her. As news of the Twin Towers falling and rumors of other planes being hijacked came on the air, my fear level rose. We were getting reports that planes were coming down all over the country. We didn't know what to believe, except that we saw enough evidence live and in color on the television screen. Of course, millions of people were trying to reach family members and friends that morning, and the phone lines were jammed. It didn't help that we were on an island with spotty service in the best of times. For six hours, I didn't know if Jen was alive or dead, but finally, my call went through and I heard her voice.

After two weeks in Curaçao, our squad returned home, but almost immediately, we were activated with orders for two years based in St. Paul, but we could be deployed at any time anywhere in the world. It couldn't have come at a worse time for my career because I was up for a big promotion and a huge raise. Whenever I started feeling sorry for myself for missing out on the big bump in my career, I remembered the three thousand men and women who perished on 9-11, people who would have been thrilled with the inconvenience of a deployment near home.

Pre 9/11 TSgts Ketterling, Cortte, Anderson, and Schmitt
(RIP Schmitty #333)

In the military, soldiers, sailors, and airmen are always on edge because they can be sent virtually anywhere at any time. Jen and I were still trying to have a baby, but I heard rumors that we might be sent to Kuwait or Saudi Arabia. I was assigned to MacDill Air Force Base, Central Command and Special Operations Command in Tampa, which was the headquarters for the war on terror. General Tommy Franks was based there, and we could tell if something bad had happened when he would smoke a cigarette outside his home. We watched the news to see what the bad news was. I was deployed to MacDill AFB in October 2001 and returned to our base in St. Paul that Christmas.

In a training accident, I broke my wrist really badly. Being immobilized in a cast wasn't enough, so the doctors performed surgery. That didn't work, so they scheduled a second operation. This time, the surgeon put metal rods in my hand, wrist, and forearm to stabilize my wrist.

After 9-11, the airline industry instituted some strict rules and procedures to prevent another hijacking. The changes complicated life for everyone who works in the industry. Not long after the attack, Jen decided to quit her job. She planned to get pregnant, and she didn't want anything to interfere.

It wasn't long before Jen was pregnant again. We were equally thrilled and anxious. What would happen this time? Our hopes were crushed again when Jen had a third miscarriage. Some miscarriages, I was learning, require medical intervention, and sometimes overworked doctors and nurses don't have the best bedside manner. A patient can feel like they're on an assembly line to be seen, treated, and sent home. I took Jen to the hospital, and this time her nurse was the most attentive, compassionate, loving person I've ever encountered. She was just what Jen needed . . . and just what I needed. I told her, "I don't even need to ask if you're a Christian. I can see Christ in you."

She smiled and told us, "Yes, I'm a believer."

I asked her what church she attended. She told us, and then she prayed for us. I'm not sure it would have meant more if an angel had come from heaven to be at Jen's bedside that day. The nurse's name is Joy.

Even with the affirmation of Joy's love and prayers in the hospital, old traumas were resurrected in our minds and hearts. My wrist hurt so much that the doctor prescribed OxyContin. Because of my history of addiction, I had to be very careful about taking opioids, but that day, I ran out of pills. I planned to call the doctor to get a refill on my prescription, but I realized that I wanted them to numb the heartache of losing our baby much more than numbing the pain in my wrist. This was a major step forward for me. I could easily have gotten a refill, and I could easily justify it because of the physical pain, but I was aware that medicating my emotional pain could put me back in my old, destructive habits. No call, no refill, no pills.

I wasn't sure it was possible to hurt more than we did after losing the first two babies, but this was even worse. I prayed, "God, if You don't want us to have children, why would You let Jen get pregnant?"

People at River Valley were praying for us. They saw us as the poster couple of a marriage God had restored, so they were faithful to hold us up in prayer. The next Sunday after the miscarriage, Jen and I struggled about going to church. This was before the days of social media, so we couldn't post an update to let everyone know of our most recent loss. We debated whether we could stand all the questions and comments when we told people we'd lost a third child, but we decided to go. We realized the damage that happened to us when we avoided spending time with God's people, especially those who know and love us. Still, it's hard to break bad news to people who love you and are praying for you. It's hard to see them cry as they share your disappointment. But I had another reservation about going to church that day: I'd been in church my whole life, and I knew people who seemed to thrive on their personal drama. They made hard times sound even worse so they could elicit pity and prayers. I bristle around people who spew negativity, and I vowed never to be the "sad story" guy. But our story *was* sad . . . in fact, *very* sad.

We walked in that morning and told a few people what had happened that week. They were very kind and supportive. We then sat in our usual place and spoke to the people all around us. As the service started, my heart was flooded with the emotions I'd felt when I sat in the back row at the depths of my addiction. I had run out the door then, and I wanted to run now. But this time I didn't run. I stayed with Jen. During the singing, we wept even as we raised our hands in worship. Couples who were in a small group with us noticed that we were crying, and during the service, they got up, came over to where we were standing, embraced us, and wept with us. Kristie Kerr, the same Kristie who saw my apartment when it was a mess, was the keyboard player in the band. When she saw us crying and our friends surrounding us with love, she left the stage—in the middle of a song—and came down to cry with us and hug us. Her husband Jeff, the worship pastor, looked at her as if to ask, "What are you doing?" But he realized she was stepping into our lives at this difficult moment, so he just rolled with it. About a dozen people huddled around us to support us in our time of sorrow. It was one of the most meaningful moments of my life.

I look back at the love poured out on us in the church service as a major turning point for Jen and me. We walked into the room totally broken, and not in a good way. If our friends hadn't shown so much support, I'm afraid I could have gone back to drinking, our restored marriage would have been torn apart, and our lives would have been Disaster 2.0, a place where returning probably wouldn't happen. We walked into the room that day on the verge of self-pity and resentment, but God used the love of our friends to soften our hearts. We were again surrendered to Him—no matter what comes.

When we got home that day, we were physically and emotionally exhausted, but we sensed that God had done something wonderful to affirm His love through our friends. Before the service, we'd been looking for answers to our questions . . . we *demanded* answers to our questions. But God calmed our hearts and gave us His peace, even without the answers. His love was enough. We walked into the church that morning feeling defeated, but now we sensed that God was in control, and we could trust Him. He is good, wise, and loving, and that's all the answer we needed. In the good times and the bad, God is faithful.

We've all heard preachers say things like, "Heartaches will either make us bitter or better," and "The same sun that hardens clay softens clay, so be clay in God's hands." Those sentences may seem trite to a lot of people, but not if they've had to look in the mirror and make the colossal choice to either let bitterness consume them . . . or discover a deeper level of trust in God than they've ever experienced before.

CHAPTER 6

AUTISTIC INTERPRETATION

The week following the transformational worship service, my sister Jennifer and her husband Eric planned to attend an informational seminar about adoption. They already had two children, but they wanted to add to their family through adoption. My sister asked me, "I don't want to overstep here. The two of you have gone through a lot, but do you and Jen want to go with us? It's just to learn more about adoption. No commitment at all."

I'm pretty sure we would have felt misunderstood and offended by the invitation coming so quickly after our crushing disappointment, but the love we experienced during the church service gave us some room to breathe. We were open to anything the Lord might have for us. We thought, *Why not?* I'm not sure what our expectations were because we were still in a kind of emotional fog, but we were open to whatever God had for us.

The four of us drove about two hours south of Minneapolis to a little town where the meeting was held. The speaker was an agency director who had a large network of contacts throughout the country, and she was very realistic about the blessings and challenges of adoption. As we listened, Jen and I each felt God prompting us that adoption was something He wanted for us. We weren't sure how to tell each other, but when we did, we were relieved that God had spoken the same message to both of us. In fact, we both felt led to ask for a transracial adoption.

When the speaker finished her presentation, we talked to her. Most of the people in the room, it turned out, were on the front side of learning about adoption. Jen and I should have been in that group, but God had spoken to us and we were ready to take the next step. She told us, "If you're looking for a blonde, blue-eyed baby girl, you'll probably need to wait between two and three years."

We told her that we weren't just open to a transracial adoption, but we both felt God leading us in that direction. She then said, "Well, if that's the case, the process will move a lot faster, maybe under two years."

We were highly motivated to fill out the paperwork. It was one of those instances where God gave us the added drive and persistence to get something done that would normally take a long time, because "you just know that you know" that you need to. There were a lot of detailed forms, background checks, references, and interviews with a social worker. Within a week, we mailed in the application and the initial paperwork. About three weeks later, we received a call that a birth mom had selected us and was going to give birth right away. We had to wait for the interstate paperwork and documentation to be completed, but only six weeks after the informational meeting south of Minneapolis, an African-American baby girl was waiting for us in Charlotte, North Carolina. We were told that this was the quickest adoption in the history of the agency.

Sometime during those weeks, we got a clearer picture of how the agency handles adoptions. They see it as a ministry to the birth mom, and they give the mother full control of the big decisions leading up to the adoption, including selecting the family that will adopt her child. She can change her mind and switch gears at any time. Prospective adoptive couples create a "picture book" showing who they are and where they live. Not to be crass, but it's an extended sales brochure. The moms review as many of these as they want to see, and then they decide. The agency continues to provide support to the birth mom years after the adoption.

The birth mom in Charlotte didn't take long. As soon as she saw the book about Jen and me, she said, "They're the ones."

We'd prayed that the process would go fast, and wow, God really answered our prayers! Now we had to scramble to finish all the forms and get them to the adoption agency. We had to be fingerprinted, and we had to rush to get our references in. We bought a crib and a rocking chair, and friends brought us tons of baby stuff they knew we'd need. I felt like we were contestants in *The Amazing Race!*

There was one more detail: the cost for the adoption was close to $15,000. We had savings for about half of that, but help came from a local church fund sponsored by families who created a network of mentoring and support for transracial adoptions and the families. Pastor John Piper called it The Micah Fund. And because I was still technically employed at my company, even though I was activated for the war on terror, I still had access to benefits. I really believe God led me to look through the Human Resources manual to discover that the company offered $5,000 toward the cost of domestic adoption! God was meeting our needs in ways we'd never imagined. What God calls for He provides for.

It was late April, 2003. For two years, we'd prayed and hoped God would give us a child, and now, suddenly, in a way we'd never expected, we were flying to Charlotte to pick up a baby—*our* baby—that we'd never seen before. After we landed, we checked into a hotel, and then we drove to the offices of the agency. Someone handed the baby girl to Jen, and we just stood there and sobbed with delight. God had answered our prayers after all.

The day was a whirlwind: flying to Charlotte, getting a rental car with car seat, driving straight to the agency, then being handed our daughter as soon we walked in. After signing the required paperwork, we sat on their couch for an hour until they finally laughed and said, "You can go now. She's yours!" We were so shocked we could have sat there all day. It finally sank in: She's ours!

We stayed at a hotel in Charlotte for a week until all the interstate adoption paperwork was filed. Those were precious days. We named our baby JoJo. We kissed her, and we kissed each other. We only stopped crying when we changed her, fed her, or caught some sleep. We flew back to Minneapolis on a Sunday morning . . . Mother's Day. By the time we got settled, it was mid-afternoon. I told Jen, "The only thing I regret is that you didn't get to stand up with all the other moms in church today." I had a key to the church and wanted to take her there right then and have her stand, but she said she was fine waiting until next year. I nodded. "But next year, you'll be standing." It was especially meaningful to her to bring our daughter home on the day to honor moms.

Shortly thereafter, I received a medical discharge from the Air Force National Guard because my wrist was permanently fused from the injury and I was deemed permanently disabled. I immediately went on staff full time at River Valley Church to work with the Recovery Ministry and Young Adults. Going into full-time ministry was a huge financial step of faith for us. Without income from Jen's job and after my departure from the collection agency and the military, our income was cut by over seventy percent. It was a big hit, but we were doing exactly what God had called us to do. All our savings had been spent on the adoption, and we were barely scraping by, but we were very happy . . . except for one thing: we were exhausted.

From the first day we brought JoJo to the hotel in Charlotte, she had a very hard time sleeping. On that first night, she wouldn't stop crying. We tried everything we knew to do. Nothing worked. Was something wrong with our baby? Were *we* doing something wrong? At one o'clock in the morning, I called a nurses hotline we'd been given earlier in the day. The nurse was calm and measured. She told me, "Mr. Anderson, babies cry. She'll be fine."

Okay, thanks.

In the next few weeks, we realized JoJo wouldn't sleep unless we were touching her, and I often put my face next to hers so she could hear me breathing. Of course, we'd never been parents before, so we vacillated between two conclusions: JoJo's problems were completely normal, or we were bad parents. When we saw friends with their babies sleeping soundly in a stroller, and we heard how this baby or that one was sleeping through the night, we leaned toward the more self-condemning conclusion. This went on day after day, night after night, month after month. Jen and I devoured books to help parents with their kids who can't sleep, but nothing seemed to work. JoJo screamed for hours, and at least one of us was up with her for many hours every night.

JoJo simply would not go to sleep in her crib. She screamed until one of us picked her up. Somehow, we needed to find some way to have JoJo sleeping in our bed at night without rolling over on her. Jen had an idea: We used one of our small roller-suitcases, zipped it open, and put blankets inside. We put it between us on the bed so JoJo would be close to us without the danger of being smothered. It wasn't a perfect solution, but it was the best one we could find.

In May 2004, when JoJo was only a year old, Jen took her to Target to buy some diapers and other things she needed. When she got home and opened the door, her face was radiant. She was filled with joy. She didn't wait for me to ask what was going on. She blurted out, "Joe, you won't believe it! God spoke to me when I was at Target!"

I was a little suspicious of her playing the "God told me" card, so I asked, "Okay, what did you buy?"

I wasn't far off. She took a onesie outfit out of her bag and informed me, "God told me that we're going to adopt a chubby little African-American baby boy!" She let that sink in for a few seconds, and then she continued,

"I just know it. I know he's out there, and I know we're going to adopt him. I know he's our son!"

I didn't want to contradict God or burst Jen's bubble, but I had to be honest with her, "Jen, we don't have any money—like zero. We're barely making it now. I don't see how we can pay for another adoption."

She was unfazed. "That's okay. God told me. He'll make it happen somehow. He's done it before, and He'll do it again."

This was a major role reversal. I'm normally the risk-taker, and Jen worries about details. I'd never seen her so filled with faith and assurance! I hoped she'd forget about it. She didn't. A week later at about 4:30 on a Friday afternoon, I was home alone when our landline rang. I assumed it was a telemarketer, so I thought about not answering. I picked it up, and to my surprise, it was someone at the adoption agency in Charlotte. She asked how we were doing with JoJo. I told her we were doing great, and then she said, "Joe, this is very unusual, and normally, we use a different process." I couldn't wait to hear her next line. "We have a birth mom who is rejecting all the prospective parents we show her. We've asked her what she's looking for, and everybody in our office agrees that she's looking for a family like yours . . . or maybe not *like* yours, but *you*. Would you be willing for us to show her your picture book?"

My head was spinning. I asked, "When is the baby due?" I wanted time to think about the offer. I hoped she was in her first trimester.

The lady explained, "Well, Joe, the thing is, she had the baby this morning."

I was stunned: "Boy? Girl? Caucasian, Latino, African-American?"

"He's an African-American boy. He has the chubbiest cheeks you ever saw."

I'm not sure she understood when I told her, "Well, there's no way this isn't going to work out! Yeah, go ahead and show her our picture book."

She said she'd call back as soon as she had a decision from the birth mom. A few minutes later, Jen came home. When I told her about my conversation, she was ecstatic! It was a promise fulfilled . . . in record time!

About two hours later, the phone rang. The lady from the adoption agency said, "She looked you over, and she said, 'They're exactly the family I was thinking of.'" The baby was put in foster care until the adoption was complete.

The paperwork required for an adoption is sometimes compared to buying a house, but it's really not that similar. It's about three times as much! There was always one more document we needed to sign. The agency wanted us to come to Charlotte as soon as possible to pick up the baby, but to say we weren't prepared is an understatement! And besides, I was scheduled to lead a missions trip with seventeen interns to Trinidad in just a few days. I called the sister agency in the Twin Cities to see how we could expedite all the paperwork. The lady there said, "You have to start from scratch. We need fingerprints and references, and you have to meet with a social worker three times before you're cleared to pick up the child." But she had a very good suggestion: "Call the social worker who handled your first adoption. She might be able to speed things along."

We called Karine, our social worker, and she told us she had planned to leave for Memorial Day weekend with her family in the Northern Woods, but for some reason, the Holy Spirit told her to stay at home. When I explained the situation, she remarked, "This is why God wanted me to stay here!" We met with her three times over that Saturday and Sunday. I took Jen to the Air Force base near us so we could be fingerprinted—on a holiday weekend. I left for the missions trip on Monday morning with some forms still not submitted. I'm not sure, but I think Jen got my best friend Ryan to sign my name on a few of them!

In Trinidad, it was difficult to get a phone line back home. I didn't know if everything had been submitted or if there were snags along the way. The birth mom could have changed her mind—which often happens. Jen told me that it looked like the agency had everything they needed. Now they were waiting for me to get back so we could fly to Charlotte.

In the rush to get everything to the agency, I'd forgotten one tiny detail: we didn't have any money for the adoption . . . or the hotel . . . or the flights.

I thought about asking my parents for a loan, but it didn't seem right. If God had spoken to Jen so clearly, surely He was going to provide the money. Word had spread that we were going to adopt another baby, and some friends called and said, "We know all this has come together really fast, and we want to let you use our miles for the flights." Great. One down, about $15,000 to go.

Jen and I drove to Walmart to buy another car seat. Before we walked in, my cell phone rang. It was someone in accounting at the local Air Force base. I'd been discharged a year earlier, so I had no idea why they were calling. She said cheerfully, "This is Sergeant So-and-so from the Accounting Department. Is this Master Sergeant Joseph Anderson?"

"Yes," I replied as Jen and JoJo waited for me on the sidewalk in front of the store.

She explained, "We've been trying to get in touch with you. Because you had a medical discharge before your enlistment was up, you're entitled to a severance payment from the Air Force."

I told her, "I'm already getting a monthly disability payment for my injury."

"This," she assured me, "is totally different. I need to know if you want the check sent in the mail as a paper copy, or if you want it by direct deposit."

I thought, *It's probably $3.00 or something close to that.* But I asked, "How much are we talking about?"

She obviously was looking at the figures. She said, "The amount is close to $21,000. After taxes, it's $17,193."

I'm sure my response shocked her. I started crying. Through my sobs, I asked her to verify that she had the right Joe Anderson, if everything was accurate, and if it was a done deal. She assured me that everything was on the level. I asked her to use direct deposit so I could get it as soon as possible, and then I thanked her profusely. When I got off the phone, I turned to Jen and yelled, "God provided the money! He just paid for our baby!"

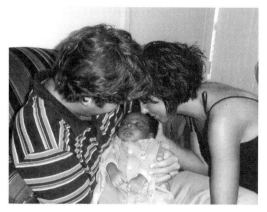

A couple of days later, Jen, JoJo, and I flew to Charlotte to pick up our son. We'd broken the record for the quickest adoption—from the first call until we held baby Joey in our arms was just three weeks. We waited a couple of days for all the paperwork to clear, and then we headed home. We were arriving back in Minneapolis on the weekend of Father's Day. Mother's Day for JoJo; Father's Day for Joey. Perfect. Jen and I had a little girl and a little boy. We were all set.

When we brought Joey into our family, we were amazed: Joey was a great sleeper. In only a couple of weeks, he was sleeping through the night, and he took naps—without fighting us—during the day when he got tired. This was a new experience for Jen and me. So, JoJo's problem with sleep wasn't us after all! But that meant . . .

We were thrown another curveball. JoJo started walking well before she was one year old, and as soon as she could stand, she ran. She was incredibly active, darting away from us. We had to keep our eyes—and at least one hand—on her all the time because she would run away from us into parking lots, into the street, and in front of people on the sidewalk. She was a lot of fun, but very impulsive. We assumed that was just part of being a spunky kid. As the months went by, it seemed that she often experienced "sensory overload" from loud noises, bright lights, quick movements, and almost anything and everything. She simply couldn't handle the normal distractions that happen a hundred times a day in a child's schedule.

A few months after we brought Joey home, Jen started feeling sick . . . in the mornings. While I was at work, she took a pregnancy test. When she was looking at the results, JoJo grabbed her cellphone from her hand, ran into the bathroom, and threw it into the toilet. Jen didn't have any way to communicate with me the entire day. After the three crushing miscarriages, Jen was cautiously hopeful, but also overwhelmed. The test was positive, and suddenly, Jen was filled with fear that she'd lose this one like the last three—plus, we already had our hands full with two babies.

When I walked in that evening, Jen was crying. She was spent, but I had no idea why. She had put the pregnancy test in a zip-lock bag, and she tossed it to me. She cried even more, and when I looked at it, I just laughed—not intending to be mean to Jen but because it seemed so absurd. I asked, "Why didn't you call me?" She then tossed me another zip-lock bag with her cellphone in it and explained, "Here's the reason. JoJo threw it in the toilet when I was looking at the test results." She wept, "I can't go through this again!" I ran up the stairs to hug her. We laughed and cried as we thanked God for another surprising blessing.

We were committed to being hopeful and full of faith the entire time. This was a real baby growing in Jen, and we refused to hedge our bets by not getting excited. We had to allow ourselves to be hurt again. We trusted God no matter what . . . and we believed, *This time is different. This time, God will answer our prayers!*

Thankfully, this time *was* different, and everything went smoothly. Regular doctor's appointments showed a healthy child was developing, and as she passed the important benchmarks, her fear subsided and joy filled her heart. We were extremely busy. The church was growing like crazy, and I was taking on more responsibilities with young adults, the recovery ministry, our internship program, preaching, and teaching. In addition, I had become the go-to guy for counseling with people in the church: marriage problems, addictions, fertility, adoption questions, and anything else people struggled with. The people on our staff team learned to say, "Just talk to Joe." I had

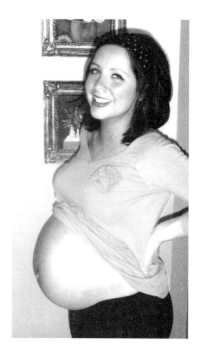

to jokingly tell the other pastors on staff, "Just because I've experienced a lot in life doesn't make me Yoda. I don't have to meet with everyone with a problem. You can give biblical advice too!"

I was excited to be in ministry, part of a growing church, and see the fruit produced in people's lives. In fact, I had a hard time turning down any opportunity to minister, so I became overcommitted. As Jen's belly grew and the due date approached, I realized it probably wasn't the wisest thing to schedule trips close to the due date, but I did anyway. I went to Zambia when Jen was almost at nine months. She was extremely supportive of my going, but on the phone call at the end of two weeks in Africa (we didn't have communication until then), I realized I should have known better. Jen was spent. I look back and wonder, *What was I thinking?*

Less than two weeks after I got home from Africa, Jada was born.

While Jen and Jada were still in the hospital, I took JoJo and Joey up to her room. Jen held Jada as I put the other two on either side of her, and I took a picture of God's three miracles.

I was scheduled to preach the Sunday after Jada was born, and I showed the picture from the hospital to introduce our newest family member. As people clapped and cheered, I could hear some of the women in the audience gasp. They saw two kids with pacifiers climbing on Jen as she held our newborn. After the service, several of them—especially those who knew how active JoJo was—told me they had mini-panic attacks as they realized how much work it would be to raise three little ones.

In twenty-three months, we went from having no children to having three little ones. Jen's parents and mine were very supportive of our rapid family expansion and helped us whenever they could.

When JoJo was almost two, we were at church at River Valley one Sunday morning, and Pastor Rob's mother, Isabel, came over to talk to us. We love her; she's like a bonus mother to Jen and me. As we talked, JoJo was her usual hyperactive self. Over ten years earlier, Pastor Rob and his wife Becca received the diagnosis that their older son Connor had autism. Isabel took a long look at JoJo, and she lovingly told us, "You probably need to have JoJo tested for autism." Jen and I instantly shook our heads. Surely it wasn't that! She's just a rambunctious little girl who will grow out of this phase of her childhood. But at the same time, we respected Isabel and knew she wasn't giving us her advice lightly.

Other people sometimes made comments about JoJo's behavior, and we were very defensive. We told ourselves that they're making those assumptions because she's adopted . . . and they've concluded that she's an African-American child who doesn't feel comfortable in our home.

Gradually, we had to face the fact that JoJo wasn't like other children. Was it autism? We didn't know, so we went to a specialist for an assessment. The doctor gave her a sleep medication to solve one of the many problems, but that night, it had the opposite effect: JoJo was wilder than ever! When we told him about her reaction the next day, he said, "Okay, sometimes that medication doesn't work on a child, and may even have the opposite of the desired effect. We'll try something else."

I wanted to yell, "This isn't a high school science experiment! Are you just guessing? Can't you get this right?"

Gradually, we were moving toward autism as the cause of JoJo's behavior. We took her to a school called PIE: Partners in Excellence, which is known for outstanding work with kids who have the condition. JoJo was only three, but we were desperate for help. We made an appointment for another assessment. As we talked to two therapists, JoJo got up and ran out the door and down the hall. I hurried out to get her and bring her back, and when I sat down, I noticed that the therapists were looking at each other and nodding. One of them asked, "Does that happen often?"

Jen told them, "All the time. No matter where we go, we have to watch her or she'll run off. And as you saw, she's fast!"

A few more tests and observations confirmed their initial suspicion that JoJo is on the autism spectrum. Even though JoJo was very young, the school accepted her into their program. It's called ABA: Applied Behavior Analysis. She attended the school for six hours a day for three years. It was very expensive, but we believed it was the best place for our little girl.

JoJo made some significant progress, but we soon realized even the best curriculum wasn't a cure. The most helpful part of her attending the school was the love, understanding, and support among the parents. We had common struggles, and we were in the trenches together.

After three years, we enrolled JoJo in a local kindergarten, but after that, she was in special education for the rest of her time in school. Today she's a young adult, but she functions intellectually at about a second-grade level. She has a speech impairment, which makes it hard to understand what she's saying, but she's also socially aware like a teenager and gets very shy because people don't understand her. She is very specific about what she likes and is the easiest person to buy gifts or food for. She's very athletic and artistic, and she's become skilled in using technology, but she sees the world in black and white, all right or all wrong, all in or all out, so nuance and synthesis aren't her strong points.

Now that JoJo is a young adult, we have to tailor our expectations—of her and of ourselves—as she enters a new stage of her life. Barring a miracle, she will live with us the rest of our lives, so we need to plan to take care of her after we're gone. Jen and I aren't afraid of the future. It's just different than what we expected. We're like any other parent of a child with special needs—we live in the tension of wanting the very best for JoJo, loving her exactly the way she is, and at the same time grieving a little everyday what might have been.

Many people have tried to share with others what it's like to have a child who is on the spectrum. One of the best is a short story by Emily Perl Kingsley called "Welcome to Holland." She starts her story: "When you're going to have a baby, it's like planning a fabulous vacation trip—to Italy. You buy a bunch of guide books and make your wonderful plans. The Coliseum. The Michelangelo David. The gondolas in Venice. You may learn some handy phrases in Italian. It's all very exciting." She continues to explain that the child's birth is like the plane ride to the wonders of Italy, but when the plane lands, "The stewardess comes in and says, 'Welcome to Holland.'"

"Holland?!?" you say. "What do you mean Holland?? I signed up for Italy! I'm supposed to be in Italy. All my life I've dreamed of going to Italy."

Gradually, it dawns on you that there are no options of now traveling to Italy, yet Holland isn't so bad. They even have Rembrandts.

But there's a problem . . . a big problem. Everyone else is going to Italy, and they're quick to tell you how wonderful it is there. You're glad for them, but it feels empty, wrong, hard. You can't help but think, *That's where I'm supposed to be!*

Kingsley concludes that the pain of being in Holland will never go away because it's the loss of a cherished dream. However, if we spend our lives shrouded in grief and might-have-beens, we'll miss the joys offered to us in Holland.[2]

Jen and I didn't want to miss any of the joys JoJo was offering us in Holland. We had to wrestle with the fact that we were going somewhere we hadn't planned to go . . . or wanted to go, yet when we saw there were no options, we decided to go all in. This is another time when we had to believe God is faithful, even when we didn't understand what He was doing. We accept all the blessings of being JoJo's parents with all the challenges, convinced that God will use both to melt our hearts and draw us closer to Him.

And along the way, He'll use our story of joy and heartache to bring wisdom and perspective to other parents of kids who aren't like the others.

**Walk for Autism; on the right,
Logan and Connor Ketterling with JoJo**

In an ironic twist to the story, not long after Jen and I got married and before we separated, Pastor Rob invited Jen's dad, who was recovering well from the gunshot, to come to Minneapolis to preach at River Valley and tell the story of God's faithfulness. Pastor Rob describes what happened that day in his book, *Fix It!* Let him tell what happened:

> After Bill shared his story, a lot of people came down to the front for Bill to pray for them. Meanwhile, I began loading up the portable equipment and packing it in the truck. Finally, Bill had prayed for the last person, and he came over to Becca and me. She was holding Connor. I thanked him for sharing his story, and he asked, "Is there anything I can pray for the two of you?"
>
> The words "more church growth and more tithing" were form-ing in my mouth, but Becca jumped in: "Our son has autism, and we want God to heal him."
>
> At that moment, my wife was like the woman who asked Jesus to heal her daughter, and when He hesitated, she told Him, "Even the dogs get the crumbs that fall from the table." Becca was that woman who wouldn't take "no" for an answer! You have to under-stand that this was way out of character for Becca. She is so gentle

and kind, but at that moment, she was a fierce mama bear. I chimed in, "Yeah, that's what we want you to pray for," but I was thinking, *Uh, I thought we'd given up on that. Remember, "Welcome to Holland"?*

Bill smiled and put his hands on Connor. After a few seconds, he said quietly, "I feel this is from the Lord: God is going to heal your son for His glory." He paused and then told us, "God has seen that you believe He's a loving God, but He's going to show you that He's a powerful God. He's going to heal your son."

At that moment, our four-year-old son, who had never made significant eye contact with us, looked up at Becca and me and said, "Hi, Mom. Hi, Dad." Like the story of Pinocchio, the boy came alive! Then he said, "Where are we going now?" He wasn't withdrawn, and he wasn't just parroting us. God had done it!

The rest of the day, Becca and I couldn't stop crying and talking. Connor was acting like every other kid his age! We were stunned. Words can't describe our joy and gratitude. We called every member of our family and all our friends who had prayed with us and for us. It was a glorious day! This wasn't just a marginal healing; Connor was completely restored.

The next morning, we took Connor to his special ed class. We called teacher Pam over and said, "Check him out."

In an instant, she could tell he had radically changed. She almost yelled, "What happened to Connor?"

Becca told her, "He was healed in church yesterday." She was thrilled!

Pam left the room to tell her boss what God had done. Her boss wanted to test Connor for autism. It took a little while, but when she was finished, she walked into the room where Becca and I were waiting. I was shocked at her words. She snarled, "This child is completely normal. He doesn't have autism. How dare you waste taxpayer money on special education for your son for the last two years!"

I replied, "Yeah, it's every parent's dream to rip the state off through special ed!" I calmed down after a couple of seconds, and then I told her, "Our son was healed by God in church yesterday."[3]

Over years later when we received the same diagnosis, we asked Bill to pray for JoJo. After all, he's the only person I know who has prayed for a child to be healed of autism, and God answered his prayer for Connor. We have an inside track because JoJo is Bill's granddaughter, but this time, God didn't heal JoJo. It's ironic because of the connections. I'm good friends with Connor Ketterling today, and because he was healed, I see how God is blessing him and using him as an amazing pastor, husband, and now father. The miracle of his healing doesn't create any jealousy or confusion because we can see God working in and through JoJo's life too.

We've prayed for her healing for twenty years, but maybe the answer to our prayers has been God changing our perspective about JoJo and her condition. She is an amazingly compassionate person—very shy, but warm-hearted. If I tell her about someone who needs prayer, she takes it to heart and prays for God's peace and power to shower down on that person. She's a gifted athlete and continues to compete in the Special Olympics.

JoJo has a hard time expressing her own feelings, but she is very understanding and empathetic about others. When driving with JoJo in the car, several things inevitably happen. She's very aware of the laws and will call us out if we're speeding or we didn't use a turn signal to change lanes. Also, when I've expressed frustration with another driver, she always says, "Maybe they're lost or scared, or they're having a bad day, or maybe they're old and not driving as well as they used to." She keeps us all in check with our heart and actions.

We don't know why God chooses to heal one person but not another. It's not the strength of the prayer or some unknown precondition we have to guess and get right before God acts. Yes, we must have faith, and yes, timing matters, but God is sovereign over all things, and He is equally inscrutable. In the early church, James was arrested by Herod and put to death with a sword. Not long after, Peter was arrested. I'm sure he expected the same fate, but as his friends prayed for him at Rhoda's house, God sent an angel to cast off the chains and lead him through the prison as the jail doors opened. Why Peter and not James? Did no one pray for James? I'm sure they did, but God has His own purposes for each of us.

Ever since the very first moment we heard about JoJo from the adoption agency, we've felt overwhelmingly honored that God chose us to be her parents. Nothing has ever changed that. In fact, even her autism has made us feel more in awe of how God has entrusted us with her life to give her every opportunity and to be blessed by her as she shows us the love of Jesus every day. Blessings and struggles—God uses all of them for our good and His glory.

CHAPTER 7

"WONDER TWIN POWERS, ACTIVATE!"[4]

The Scriptures tell us that children are like arrows in a quiver, and with three little children, Jen and I felt like our quiver was full! The three were so close in age that they seemed like triplets. I enjoyed my role as an associate pastor at River Valley Church, but as I had opportunities to tell the story of our wedding, the shooting, our estrangement, my alcoholism and recovery, our reconciliation, adopting two babies, and giving birth to Jada, God seemed to bless this ministry. I was getting enough calls to speak at other churches that Jen and I felt God leading us to leave River Valley, and I became an evangelist for two years. God used our story of hurt and hope to touch people and change lives. It was a wonderful experience. We started Surrender Ministries and created a video of our story to share with people all across the country and even in other nations around the world. We've had the privilege of having an impact on thousands of people with the message of hope through surrendering to Jesus Christ.

After two years as an evangelist, I received a call to be the Lead Pastor at Summit Church in St. Paul, an eighty-five-year-old church in the historic area of the city. It was a church revitalization project, and we were excited to be there. I took that position in 2012 and served there for eight years. We saw amazing growth and learned a lot about what to do (and not do) in pastoring and leading people. The people of Summit Church will always have a special place in my heart.

Our three children were a handful, especially since one was a special needs child, but Jen and I always kept a door open for another adoption. God used us to encourage, guide, and support other parents as they've adopted more than a hundred children. It was part of our identity. The agencies in Minneapolis and Charlotte used pictures of our family on fliers and promotional material. Another agency somehow found our picture and used it on a banner at one of their events. We were literally the poster family for adoption!

At least one light moment stands out during this time. Jen brought home a book called *Matthew Was Adopted*. In the story, the little boy Matthew was adopted twice: once by his parents and again by God when he accepted Christ. Jen thought it would be helpful for the book to stimulate conversation about this issue in our family. When we read it, Joey picked on Jada and said, "We're like Matthew. We've been adopted twice, but you've only been adopted once by God!"

Jada started crying. She told Joey and us, "I want to be adopted twice, too!" It was funny, and kind of sweet, that she had more of a complex about not being adopted than the others did about being adopted.

One night when we were praying with Jada, she startled us when she said, "I'm praying that we'll adopt twin baby boys."

I thought, *That's so cute.* But it wasn't a passing idea. Jada prayed every night that God would lead us to twin boys. I had always loved the idea of having twin boys—the wrestling, sports, joking, and fun. What could be better?

After two months of Jada knocking on the door of heaven, I got a message from a friend who, with her family, attended our church years earlier. She wrote, "I don't want to be too forward, but we're on a mission trip in Haiti, and we're working with an orphanage. There are twin boys here, and every time I hold them, I sense that God wants them to be your boys. I don't know if you and Jen are thinking about adopting again, but the twins don't have a family. Are you at all interested?"

I thought, *You've got to be kidding!* I showed Jen the message, and we agreed to at least find out more about the boys. Through more messages, we learned their birthday is April 5, the same as Jada's, five years later. The boys were born soon after the massive earthquake in Haiti in 2010. Sadly, it was a chaotic time for a country already in crisis. Parents who had died or been displaced because of the earthquake left children in dire need. The orphanages had an influx of children.

The more Jen and I prayed and talked, the more we sensed a green light from God. We were sure the adoptions would happen really quickly, because, well, that's how it works with us. But God was whispering, "Not so fast." Haiti had just agreed to comply with The Hague Convention rules for international adoptions. The regulations were intended to stop sex trafficking and fraudulent adoptions, but for a third-world country like Haiti, where administrative systems were already primitive, the additional red tape was almost a death blow to adoptions. The most obvious unintended consequence was making families wait a year longer than normal. Of course, we didn't expect things to move slowly. The people at our church were as excited as we were, and they often asked when Jen and I were going to fly to

Haiti so we could bring the boys home. "Not long," I often told them. "Just a few more hoops to jump through." That, I discovered over the long, grueling process, was just wishful thinking.

I may have been reading about Samson's Nazirite vow to not cut his hair, but whatever the genesis of the idea, I decided to make my own vow before God not to shave my beard until we brought the boys home. For the first few months, I looked pretty good; a few months later, I looked like I'd been trapping furs in the Rockies for a long season; and after two years without the call that all the paperwork was finished, I looked like a rabbi straight from Jerusalem.

I used my beard as a means to avoid having to answer questions every week about when we were picking up the boys. It worked out well because the older ladies who disliked my beard were the ones who were most likely to spend time in prayer asking God to hurry the process. I told them, "If you want me to shave, pray harder that God will open the door for us to pick up the twins! If you see me still with my beard, we haven't gotten an answer yet. If the beard is gone, that's the signal that Jen and I are headed to Haiti." Avoiding conversations and asking for prayer—I was killing two birds with one beard.

The wait was really frustrating. The delays weren't all about the same issues. Sometimes we were sent "one more form to fill out." Other times the regulations would change, or officials in Haiti would lose our documents, or something else entirely. We were told over and over again, "Just one more month," "We just need the last document," or "We'll let you know next week that it's done." During this time, our planning was a moving target: I was trying to get my graduate degree, but if we were traveling in the next few weeks, maybe I should delay starting a class. We had three children who were growing up. Would it be harder to integrate the twins into our family as our other three got older? Our house was pretty comfortable with three children, but we might need to think about more space with five. Should we move now or wait until they come? We also heard horror stories about what was happening at the orphanage. Social services in the country are at a minimum, so the orphanage operates at a bare-bones level. We heard that dysentery had ravaged the kids, and one of them died. What communicable illness would happen next? Who would die? The uncertainty hung over us like a dark cloud. If the authorities in Haiti had told us at the beginning that the process would take two and a half years, we almost certainly would have known this wasn't for us. We knew the first two to three years with a child is crucial to attach, and as the months slipped by, we realized the climb to build those attachments was getting steeper by the day.

We had an opportunity to visit the orphanage so we could at least meet the boys, begin to attach with them, and complete some of the in-country paperwork and requirements of the local courts. It was a good way to get some face-to-face time with them. While Jen and I were in Miami waiting for our flight, I got a call that our dear friends on staff with me, Levi and Kelly Hoyt, had just given birth to their beautiful baby girl Kadence Love, but she tragically passed away just after delivery. This couple meant so much to us. I'd led each of them to the Lord, baptized them, and discipled them. I felt crushed and helpless. I wanted to catch a flight back to be with them, but we had to go to Haiti to complete the paperwork. It was another moment when joy and eager anticipation was replaced with heartache.

At the orphanage, I quickly noticed that one of the twins, Jimmy, was the only child who wasn't very thin. In fact, he was a bit chubby. I wondered what the story was there. Over those few days, I found the answer. When no one was watching him closely, he would crawl under a gate and run into the kitchen. In a minute, he'd come out with a bottle of Pedialyte, which was given to the kids who were dehydrated or sick. Another time I saw him slink away from the other kids and tug on the apron of a cook. She reached down and gave him a piece of chicken. I had no idea how often Jimmy pulled stunts like this, but it was obvious that he was running the show—he was like an inmate running the prison. I was impressed and thought, *This kid is an Alpha dog!* When Jen and I left, we had a whirlwind of emotions—hopeful that we'd get our twins soon and heartbroken to see them stuck there.

It took more than two years for the adoption papers to be completed. The boys were almost one when we began, and they were three when we finally picked them up. When we finally got the word, the day set for us to go to Haiti was at the end of the Assemblies of God General Council, our denomination's biannual gathering, which was held in Orlando that year. We took our whole family to the conference. We took the kids to Disney World, and we asked Bill and JoAnne, who were there for the council, to stay with our three while Jen and I flew to Haiti to get the twins. We would fly back to Orlando and then on to Minneapolis as one big, happy family. The timing was perfect.

Jen and I took the flight from Orlando to Port-au-Prince where we boarded a small plane to fly over the mountains to Cap-Haitien, a town on the central northern coast. The plane looked like it might not make it off the runway, much less over a mountain range, but we got on board.

The plan was to stay for a couple of days so the boys would get used to us. They weren't babies any longer. In fact, they didn't even know they were twins. It took us a while to realize this fact, but then it made perfect sense. They're fraternal, not identical, and they'd been with thirty or forty kids their age since they were born. The concepts of brother and sister, mom and dad, were foreign to them. Each one thought the other was just another kid in the orphanage. We named them Jimmy and Johnny—just like the brothers James and John, the Sons of Zebedee, the "Sons of Thunder." These were perfect names for the "Sons of The Pastorizer"!

Before we left Cap-Haitien, we asked someone to drive us to a nearby village to meet the twins' birth father. We took a translator along so we could communicate with him. We wanted to know as much about the boys' background as possible. His home was just a hut with a dirt floor, and he had few possessions. When we asked him about the birth, he explained that Johnny was born first, and instead of Jimmy coming along only minutes later, the second delivery took four more hours. Their mother was in intense pain all that time. The midwife caring for her had a dual role of witch doctor, so the births involved a variety of blessings, curses, and bargains with spirits. Voodoo is the national religion of Haiti, but just as some people call the United States a "Christian nation," not everyone in either country practices the national religion. We discovered, though, that people in this village were passionately committed to voodoo.

We later learned of a voodoo god called Marasa, who comes in the form of twin boys; the first boy born will be blessed and the other cursed. Most parents in the world may consider the birth of twin boys as a blessing from God, but the Haitians consider it an evil curse—they're terrified of Marasa.[5]

The boys' father told us that when Jimmy was born (revealing that they were twin boys and not a boy and a girl), their mother went berserk. She started screaming and threatening to kill both boys, and she threw rocks at anyone who tried to protect them. She also said she was going to harm herself. Then, she ran out screaming and never came back. The father's summary statement about the mother was simple, yet stunning: "She's crazy." I'm sure he meant it in the literal sense of the word. Jen and I believe she had been captivated by a demonic influence.

In desperation, their father's mother tried to breastfeed the boys so they wouldn't die of starvation, but she couldn't produce milk for them. He knew they wouldn't last long without nourishment, so he took them in his arms and found a ride to the orphanage. It was their only chance of survival.

As he told us the story, it was obvious that he was heartbroken. He had a tender heart toward the boys, but he was so poor that he couldn't afford baby formula, even if it had been available after the chaos of the earthquake. He visited the boys from time to time during the three years before we flew to Haiti to get them. As we finished our conversation in his little home, we assured him that we would take good care of them. We prayed for him and for the boys, and we left to drive back to the orphanage.

When it was time to leave with our sons, we gathered all the paperwork and other information the orphanage gave us. The director warned us that the adjustments for three-year-olds was much different than newborns. She probably had no idea how different.

(There are specific differences between bonding and attachment. Bonding is fairly superficial and transactional, but attachment is unconditional love between a parent and child that makes a family a healthy family, so it's possible to bond without becoming attached. That's the key to Reactive Attachment Disorder and similar problems. America doesn't have orphanages anymore and prefers foster care. The orphanage in Haiti is a Christian organization with wonderful people who are aware of this problem. To promote healthy attachments, they are building houses for families to live there and care for just a few children at a time to help "foster attachments.")

If anything, the little plane sitting on the runway to take us back to Port-au-Prince was even more sketchy than the one that brought us. Some interior panels were missing, and wires hung from the sides. It looked like maintenance hadn't been a priority since the Nixon administration. And the pilot . . . he was an American who appeared to have just come off the beach. His shirt was untucked, he smoked a cigarette, and he hadn't shaved in a few days. As we took off, he told us to look over the mountains and toward the horizon—a huge storm was approaching! Jen was a flight attendant, and I was in the Air Force. We'd been through some pretty ugly weather, but this was the worst.

Through the rain and wind, we made it to the country's major airport, and we had a six-hour layover. For reasons we didn't understand until we learned more about Marasa, people who spoke to us in the airport seemed more than a little wary of being near us. They may not have been true believers in voodoo, but they knew enough to keep their distance. One lady, though, didn't stay away. She kept talking and pointing at the boys. She pointed at Johnny and said, "That little one loves you." Then she pointed at Jimmy and said, "You'd better watch out for that one. He's going to cause you trouble." She then laughed and walked away. Jen was disturbed and offended.

When we arrived in Miami, we went through customs, and the boys instantly became American citizens due to the rules regarding international adoptions. It was late at night. Because of all the delays, the airline put us up at a hotel at the airport so we could relax and get some sleep before going to Orlando for a few days to be with JoJo, Joey, Jada, and the grandparents before our flight back to Minneapolis. The boys behaved well. After all, they'd been in a very regimented system their entire lives, so they knew to follow the rules, even if our rules weren't very demanding. But of course, leaving the only home they'd ever known and being taken on plane flights with adults they barely knew made them feel uncomfortable and afraid.

And we're white. Over time, my view of short-term missions to visit orphanages has changed. It's often much more disruptive than the visitors can imagine. Unless teams are careful, getting the classic missions trip picture with an orphan for their social media page does terrible damage to the child by reinforcing bonding to get candy or affection. Children who are visited fairly regularly by Westerners (typically white people) associate a white face with handfuls of candy, so they immediately run up to them with their hands open. We got our first glimpse of this phenomenon in the airports in

Port-au-Prince and Miami when the boys went up to every white person they saw, pulling on their leg, expecting a hug and a handout. This, we found out, is a symptom of a problem too often seen in orphanages: kids become skilled at creating transactional bonds to get something they want, but they're deficient in creating meaningful human-to-human attachments. In foster care, attachments form much more readily (even though it's still difficult when a child is taken from one home to another), and the pain of being adopted and losing one attachment is compensated by forming new ones. Like the roots of a plant that grow deep and strong, even if it's uprooted it can be replanted and grow. In contrast, a shallow root system makes a plant very vulnerable. That's the difference between attachment and bonding.

When we arrived in Minneapolis, we were a family of seven. Immediately, Johnny began acting out. Later we realized this was a very good sign because he was grieving the loss of familiarity at the orphanage. He told us from time to time that he wanted to go back where he felt more comfortable, he knew everyone, and he knew the system. Jimmy was very happy in his new environment—he wasn't grieving any losses because he hadn't felt any meaningful connections with the other kids or the staff at the orphanage.

When we took the twins to sporting and other events for our other three, Johnny acted like any other kid; he wandered around looking for things that interested him. But Jimmy played the crowd. Like a master politician trying to impress voters, he walked up to people, introduced himself, repeated their names, gave eye contact, and held a conversation for a minute or two. People were amazed at the verbal and relational skills of this three-year-old.

About six months after we brought the twins home, I was scheduled to go on a mission trip to Cambodia. A month before I left, Jen told me about some strange things that had happened with Jimmy when I was at work. She told me about several violent outbursts of temper, and then he acted like it never happened. Jen shook her head and told me, "It seems, well, demonic to me."

I was convinced she was exaggerating. Jen had been wrestling with five little kids, homeschooling the ones who were older, and chasing after the little ones. She was exhausted, and Jimmy's little tantrums seemed much bigger than they really were. "You just need a break," I assured her. "It's nothing. I'm sure of it." At least, that's what I told her was probably happening. She didn't buy it.

But then I witnessed some odd things too. At one point, out of the corner of my eye I saw Jimmy pick up some sunglasses and tear them apart. When I confronted him, he denied it. Then there were several instances of things in the house being broken or missing, and Jimmy knew about all of them, even if he wasn't at home at the time. It was really odd. One day after he broke something and denied it, I sat him  in a chair and did my dad thing to talk sense into him, and before my eyes, his entire demeanor changed. This tough little boy suddenly became very feminine, and he stuck his tongue in and out like a snake. Even more, he seemed very satisfied that I was upset with him, like he'd won—he had me. I was freaked out.

Jen and I prayed for and with Jimmy. It was obvious to us that something was very different about this child. I told Jen that I didn't think I should go on the trip to Cambodia, but she assured me, "I'm just glad you're finally seeing what I've been seeing for quite a while. Go, we'll be fine."

I decided to go. To prepare, I went into our basement to get my suitcase, and I took Jimmy with me. He seemed genuinely afraid to go down there, which was totally out of character for a kid who always seemed to have life by the tail. I noticed his reaction, but I didn't think much of it.

The multiple flights to Phnom Penh took about thirty hours. As soon as I got to our hotel and got on the internet, I received an email from Jen that made my blood run cold. When she got up the first morning after I left, before any of the children were up, she noticed a number of things in the house that had been broken during the night. There had been, as far as she could tell, no noise associated with the damage. Nothing had caused her to wake up. Video games were smashed. Every computer screen and television had deep scratches; about twenty leather shoes, owned by everyone in the family, had been cut to pieces. Track ribbons won by JoJo and Jada had been cut, the glass in pictures was broken, and chunks of Joey's hair had been cut—and not just a few ends, he had a bald spot on his head, but it hadn't woken him up.

Jen was alarmed. Four of the kids were crying because some of their favorite things had been desecrated, but Jimmy just sat and laughed. He told them, "I did it, and none of you even woke up!" Remember: he's now four years old.

A little later, Jen walked down to the basement to see if there was any damage there. It was a mess—a lot of things had been smashed. He had used a spare blade for a circular saw on things we were storing, but he had been expert enough to avoid cutting himself. Paint cans had been opened and turned over, and a box of ammunition I'd hidden was now out in the open. Upstairs and downstairs, a total of about two hundred things had been broken, cut, or badly scratched.

Jen's mom arrived that day to help with the kids while I was on the missions trip to Cambodia. Jen called our pediatrician to tell her what had happened, and she was alarmed. She told Jen to take Jimmy to the children's hospital. JoAnne was very somber, "This is really bad. I'm glad you're taking him to see a specialist."

I got on the first flight out of Cambodia. As soon as I arrived in Minneapolis, I went to the hospital to see Jimmy. Jen was at home with the other kids. The hospital requires visitors to register at the reception desk, but there was a problem: the line was moving really slowly. I pleaded with the receptionist to let me go ahead because my son was in crisis. He shook his head. I felt like he enjoyed having power over people, especially me at this moment. He said, "Sir, you'll just have to wait your turn." My impatience got the best of me. I bolted from the line, ran up several flights of stairs, and went directly to Jimmy's room. The receptionist called a "code," and security guards came into the room to arrest me. The nurse vouched for me, and one of the guards sneered, "Okay, but don't ever do that again."

I soon learned that Jimmy had been at his charming best in the hospital, but the physicians could tell they were dealing with a little boy who was very disturbed and manipulative.  They recommended the pediatric psychiatric unit at the Mayo Clinic in Rochester, Minnesota, but we soon learned their minimum age is six. I got on the phone and pleaded with the clinic admissions specialist to accept Jimmy. I told her that Jimmy is as smart as most six year olds, and she agreed to let him come.

I followed the ambulance for the two-hour drive to Rochester. Jen stayed with the other four at home. Jimmy was admitted for a week of testing, and I got a hotel room so I could be with him every day. The tests showed what we already knew—he was off the charts in intelligence and problem-solving skills.

On the last day, I met with the psychiatrist and the team that had been conducting the battery of tests. The doctor told me, "We're diagnosing Jimmy with Reactive Attachment Disorder. He needs to know his value and his worth. He's fighting against it, and he's rejecting love and offers of attachment. That's why most of his acting out is directed toward his mother." That made sense of why the worst behavior happened when I was at work or on trips. The doctor then told me, "The very best clinic to help children like Jimmy isn't far from your home. It's in the Twin Cities. The therapy will seem counterintuitive: for instance, he cuts up shoes, so give him more shoes." Counterintuitive? Absolutely. Desperate enough to try anything? No doubt.

I found out that the clinic is run by a husband and wife team who are both psychologists. When I called and explained what had happened that night when Jimmy ransacked the house, the husband told me, "Oh, you need to talk with my wife Dr. Amanda. She's an expert at this kind of problem." I made an appointment for our initial visit.

As Jimmy and I drove back from Rochester, I realized it would be too much of a shock—maybe not for Jimmy, but for everyone else in the family—to just bring him back to the place where he'd caused so much destruction. I got a hotel room, we swam in the pool, had dinner, and tried to get a good night's sleep before we went back to the house the next morning.

At the hotel, Jimmy went to sleep in one bed, and I was awake watching television in the other. Things had been very quiet for thirty or forty-five minutes, and then Jimmy jumped out of bed and ran into the bathroom. I went in to see what was going on, but when I opened the door, I didn't see him. I pulled the shower curtain back. He wasn't there. When I turned around and looked back into the room, Jimmy was sleeping in his bed. What in the world just happened? I know I saw him get up and run into the bathroom, and I was right behind him. I wasn't sleepwalking, and I wasn't hallucinating. I'd never experienced anything remotely like this, but then, I'd never been around anyone like Jimmy. It was a really creepy moment. I began to think of all the times when something got broken in another room while Jimmy was sitting at the kitchen table, and he admitted that he had made it happen. I vacillated between, *How is this even possible?* and, *Am I losing my mind?*

When we got home the next morning, Jen and I moved Johnny to another room, and we put an alarm on Jimmy's door so we'd know if he got out of his room. Thankfully, our counseling appointment was just a couple of days after Jimmy and I returned home. The therapist, Dr. Amanda, first met with Jen. While they met, Jimmy and I sat in the waiting room. As he played with Legos, I looked at him and wondered, *How did this little boy destroy so much in our house, especially with no one hearing a thing?* It was inconceivable to me.

When Jen came out, I met with Dr. Amanda to give my point of view, and then she put Jimmy through a battery of tests. The results were the same as the Mayo Clinic: Jimmy is very smart, and he has very good fine motor skills, but he definitely has Reactive Attachment Disorder. Dr. Amanda asked Jen and me to come to her office so she could go over the results. After she read the report, she looked at us solemnly and said, "When children have a psychological problem, it usually shows up in these results, but I see no overt indication of any other problem. I'm a Christian, and Joe, I know you're a pastor. He definitely needs therapy, but the things he's done are beyond his limitations. Therapy will only go so far. We can start the therapy right away, but I truly believe he needs an exorcism."

Her analysis shocked me. I blurted out, "Whoa, wait just a minute! Let me wrap my head around this. I was in Cambodia and got an urgent message from Jen about all the destruction in our home. I flew back, we took Jimmy to the Mayo Clinic, and the people there recommended we bring him to you. And you're saying he's demon possessed? It can't be. He's a Christian. We pray over him. He prays. He can quote passages of Scripture. None of this makes any sense!"

She wasn't surprised at my reaction. She patiently explained, "Reactive Attachment Disorder is definitely a psychological problem. Children who suffer from it are obsessed with fire, sharp objects, blood, gore, murder, and death. Sometimes there's a demonic influence in the disorder. I can almost guarantee that he has been visited by 'an imaginary friend' in the orphanage. Bright, observant children in orphanages are more aware of their sense of abandonment, and they're open to having an imaginary friend keep them company. The friend usually has dark skin and red eyes. It's a demon. With the aid of this friend, the child can find extra food and other things to make life a little less empty."

It all seemed too bizarre to believe, but I certainly couldn't make sense of Jimmy's behavior any other way. I thought about his uncanny ability to navigate the orphanage and get extra food whenever he wanted it. The pastors in our district were beginning a three-day prayer and fasting retreat, and it was starting that night. I hadn't planned to attend because I was supposed to still be in Cambodia, and now I was caught up in Jimmy's problems, but I thought, *What better place could there be for me to take him?*

As Jen and I drove home, we had an overwhelming sense that we needed to take a hard look at our lives and make sure everything was right with God. Instantly, both of us knew what we needed to focus on. A couple of years earlier, Pastor Rob and I had a falling out . . . a big falling out, and Rob's wife Becca and Jen had been caught up in the distrust and anger. The Holy Spirit brought this up to both of us at the same time, and almost in unison, we said, "We've got to make this right! We can't give the devil a foothold of resentment." I wasn't sure how, but I was committed to talk to Rob as soon as possible.

I called Pastor Clarence, our District Superintendent. I told him what had been going on, and I asked, "Can I bring both boys to the retreat for us to pray for them?"

"Absolutely!" he replied. "We'll gather some people to pray for the boys and your whole family. Bring them tonight." I didn't plan to bring everybody . . . just Jimmy and Johnny. If Jimmy had been visited by a demon in the orphanage, I thought it was possible Johnny had too.

As we drove home from the clinic, it was early afternoon, so I had only a few hours before I needed to head north. I wanted to probe this idea about an imaginary friend without being too obvious. I asked Jen to join us, and I began, "Jimmy, your mom and I have lots of friends. You know a lot of them, don't you?" He nodded, so I continued, "Do you have any friends your mom and I haven't met?"

He looked at me like I was stepping over a line, so I assured him, "You're not in any trouble. Does your friend that we don't know have, oh, let me see, blue eyes like me?"

"No."

"Well, does he have green eyes like your mom?"

"No."

"How about brown eyes like yours?"

"No."

"Hmmm. Then what color are his eyes?"

"Red."

Jen and I caught each other's gaze. We were thinking the same thing, *How did it happen that our little boy had a relationship with a demon?*

Like most pastors, I hadn't had much experience with overt demonization. The devil's schemes to tempt? Certainly. Deceive? Of course. Accuse? Yes. But not this. I'd prayed often that Jesus would bind the enemy in a person's life, and in the world of addiction, Satan's influence was obvious. Somehow, this was different.

Later that afternoon, I told Johnny and Jimmy to hop in the car. I explained again that we were going to a retreat for the night. About halfway there, as the sun was going out of sight and the sky was turning dark, Johnny started rocking back and forth, which was one of the self-soothing techniques he'd acquired in the orphanage anytime he became nervous or sensed danger. At the same time, Jimmy became very intense and asked, "Where are we going?" "Who's going to be there?" "Do we have to go?" To be honest, I was getting scared of who or what was riding in the car with us.

At that moment, my cellphone rang. Jen had called a number of women in the church to come over and pray that God would do something at the retreat to free Jimmy from Satan's bondage. She told me, "Joe, I don't know what happened, but when your mom came to the door, the power went out at our house. I checked the circuit breakers. They're all fine. What should we do?"

"Just keep praying," I pleaded with her.

Jen called the women to tell them to come even though the front lights were out. Together, they called down the love and power of God to free Jimmy. In the car, the intensity increased . . . I could almost cut it with a knife. I looked in the rearview mirror to check on the boys. Johnny was still rocking. Something was really bothering him; he could sense the warfare. At one point, Jimmy glared at me with hate in his eyes, and his face looked demonic. I turned around for a second to give him eye contact, and his face changed to a pleasant smile. It was like he was shape-shifting every time I looked at him. I wasn't sure we were going to make it to the retreat center. I'd had praise and worship music playing since we got in the car. I hoped it would soothe all of us. At that moment, a song by Hillsong came on: "Jesus' Blood." The refrain is "Jesus' blood never fails me." I turned to Jimmy and said, "Son, sing this with me." I sang a line or two, and I listened for Jimmy's voice. I heard in a raspy voice, "Jesus' blood *always* fails me."

I yelled, "No! I rebuke that in Jesus' name! Jesus' blood *never* fails me!" It was the most intense spiritual warfare I've faced in my life (up to that point). I had goosebumps and the ominous feeling that evil personified was riding in the car with us.

As soon as we stopped in the campground parking lot, Johnny stopped rocking and Jimmy turned into a sweet little boy. What would these pastors think when they saw how well-behaved these children are, while their dad is a basket case? It reminded me of taking a car to a mechanic, only to have the strange engine noise stop just before you get there.

The boys and I walked into the building, and when we turned a corner, I literally bumped into Pastor Rob. Both of us were surprised. The only thing more explosive than two UFC fighters running into each other backstage before a title fight is two feuding pastors running into one another at a ministry event. Funny, but true. Pastor Rob looked at me wide-eyed, as if he wondered how I might act. It almost never worked out in his schedule that he could come to this annual event, but there he was—only hours after the

Spirit had directed me to make things right with him. This was it. This was the moment the Spirit had prepared for me.

Tears came to my eyes, and I told him, "I'm so glad to see you. I'm here because—I know this sounds crazy—one of my twin boys has demons. I want you to know that I can't live with our relationship being so strained. I want to reconcile with you. Please forgive me for the hurt I've caused you, and I forgive you for hurting me. Pastor Rob, I love you. I'm not sure how it came to this point, but I want us to be friends." I was crying, Rob was crying, and we hugged for a long time. It was a God moment that had far more meaning than just the words that were said. But it took a face-to-face encounter. I don't think an email or even a phone call would have meant so much.

Rob told me, "I'll be praying for you and Jimmy. Let's get together again and talk as soon as we can." (A week later, Rob, Becca, Jen, and I met. We talked, prayed, and closed that ugly chapter of our lives. I asked Pastor Rob to lead an extended child dedication for Johnny and Jimmy, with Scripture, prayer, and communion. It was a beautiful and powerful time for all of us . . . except Jimmy. It seemed the demons were on alert against anything that pointed him to God. He manifested and attacked Jen in the middle of the dedication.)

At the campground, Pastor Clarence asked eight pastors to meet with us and pray. By then it was about ten o'clock. As we began, one of the men who had the most experience in deliverance asked the boys some questions. It became obvious that Johnny didn't have any problem with demons, so someone took him to another room to play with toys while the rest of us focused on Jimmy. For a couple of hours, the pastors asked questions, and we prayed. Through it all, Jimmy was a perfect gentleman. It was one of those times when all the right words are spoken but there's a nagging sense that something just isn't right. When we ended well after midnight, we were all very confused, and I was deeply discouraged. This, I was sure, had been our best shot at a breakthrough deliverance. If these men and women of God couldn't unlock the cell door to Jimmy's soul, what would we do?

I decided to drive back home that night. When we finally got back at about six o'clock in the morning, I was utterly exhausted. I put Jimmy in his room, and I lay down next to him and went to sleep. I had a dream: I was in a waiting room, and a seductive woman came in and sat next to me. I told her, "Get away from me!" and instantly, she disappeared. I decided to leave, but when I went out into the hall, I saw her. When our eyes met, she turned into a hideous demon and started chasing me. In my dream, as I ran from the demon lady, I could feel my heart beat slower and slower, as if my blood flow was cut off and I was about to pass out. At that moment, I woke up. My heart was beating so hard that I could feel it in my ears. But that's not all. Jimmy was still sound asleep, face down, with his body completely relaxed, but his hand was clamped on my neck on my artery. My heart was pounding so hard to keep the blood flowing to my brain! I quickly pried his hand off my throat. I could feel the blood rushing back into my brain just before I was about to pass out. I was okay, but to be honest, in shock and totally creeped out by what just happened. That morning, I wasn't at all sure what had happened during the night. It all seemed like one bad dream after another—whether I was asleep or not.

Later that day, one of my best friends, Bill Ziemke, came to our house to check on the power outage from the night before. He's one of those people who has seen a lot in his life, and he can fix anything . . . and I mean anything. When he checked the light switch, a huge spark arced out. He exclaimed, "Did you see that!"

"Yeah," I replied. "I couldn't miss it. What happened?"

"I don't know," he shook his head as he told me. "That *can't* happen. The power was off."

At the same time, Jen was in our family room yelling for help when we heard a maniacal laugh and a voice that warned, "I'm going to hurt you and Bill." It was Jimmy. Bill followed me into the family room. For the next few minutes, the demon manifested. Jimmy screamed, and he yelled at us in another voice. His brown eyes had turned black. Bill and I prayed. Jen called my parents and some friends to pray with us, and a couple of our Christian neighbors came over. One of them has a conservative Baptist background—they aren't usually on the cutting edge of demonic encounters. He prayed fervently.

We prayed for hours. Our other kids were on their knees asking God to deliver their brother. Johnny was watching wide-eyed as the demons manifested through Jimmy. He lunged out and tore pages from the Bible, screamed at the top of his lungs, and his breath smelled like sulfur. (I know you find this unbelievable. So did I.) Johnny kept saying, "Jimmy, why are you doing this? Stop trying to bite Mommy!" We used this moment to solidify Johnny as a Christ-follower. I told him, "Johnny, we all have a choice to serve Jesus or to follow darkness. Do you reject all of this evil and only want to serve Jesus?"

Through his tears, he responded, "Yes, I want to live for Jesus only!" It was a big moment for Johnny, just as it was for all of us when we saw the reality of the spiritual world. Like Jesus said, "No one can serve two masters."

At one point, our prayers were reaching a crescendo of intensity, and it felt like something was about to leave Jimmy's body. By this point, we had been praying for several hours. It was well past ten o'clock. The lights were out in the front, and the only light in our neighborhood were the street lights. At that moment, the doorbell rang. I immediately discerned that it was a distraction, so I told Jen, "Don't go to the door." But the doorbell kept ringing over and over again. Jen decided to go to the door in case it was someone coming to pray with us. It was a man holding a package and a flashlight. He said, "Hey, I know this isn't the right address, but can you tell me where I can find this house?" He pointed to the address on the package.

Jen didn't recognize the address, but the fact that he showed up at this critical moment frustrated her. She told him, "No! It's after ten o'clock!"

He told her, "Oh, okay. That's alright." He turned and ran back to his car.

While the man was at the door, I watched Jimmy. He looked anxious, like this was his best chance to escape. I kept him close, and soon the drama of the doorbell was over. But the man was, in fact, a huge distraction. We had been, I believe, on the edge of a breakthrough, but it didn't happen. Just as true believers' steps are directed by the Lord and we find ourselves in situations being used by the Lord, unbelievers can have their steps directed by the Satan. Darkness or light—no in-between. I suspect the man got back in his car and didn't even realize how he had just been used by Satan. He probably left and wondered why in the world he stopped at that house.

After a while, Jimmy's manifestation stopped. I walked out with our Baptist neighbor and asked him, "What did you think of all that?"

He looked at me and said, "Joe, I've never seen anything like it. That's demonic!"

Jen and I had called a lot of people that night to ask them to pray. At the end of the night, Melody Skoog, a family friend who does a ton of missions work around the world, told us, "I know what you're going through. I hate to tell you this, but you need to unlearn everything you think you know about deliverance. Americans think you can just pray in Jesus' name and it's over, but this kind of demon is trying to wear you out. It's a war of attrition. There will be a lot of confusion and what looks like failed prayer. You need to learn to bind the demon in Jesus' name and go to bed. You'll fight the same fight tomorrow, and you'll need your rest."

It seemed like totally crazy advice, but I had no choice but to take her word for it, so I looked at Jimmy and said, "I bind you in Jesus' name."

He said, "Okay," and went to bed.

That was the first night in our two-year spiritual war of attrition.

CHAPTER 8

"THAT'S TOTALLY RAD, DUDE"

It was the middle of September 2014. Jen and I stripped Jimmy's room of everything but his bed and pillow, and we took everything out of the closet so he had nothing to break or throw. Every night before bed, I searched him the same way I'd search someone I was detaining as an Air Force cop, but even with such thoroughness, we still found nails and tacks in his room. They weren't just collectables. He stuck a tack in our dog. One morning we found about twenty nails, tacks, and needles in the side of his mattress. We found children's books with razor-sharp shards of glass between the pages. One day when he was manifesting, Jen saw him pick up his mattress and launch it against the wall. He was a four-year-old with the strength of a middle linebacker.

It felt like we were living in a real-life haunted house night after night. Jen and I were scared, our other four children were scared and slept in our bedroom, and even our dog was scared of Jimmy. We played worship music nonstop every day. It reminded us of God's love, power, and faithfulness, but it didn't make a dent in Jimmy's heart.

At this point in our saga, we didn't get out in public very often, for obvious reasons. But one of Jen's favorite traditions is to have the kids' pictures taken with Santa Claus every year, so we took all the children to the mall and stood in line. Every time we went out with Jimmy it always felt like we were on the front line of spiritual warfare in the unseen world . . . on edge for anything strange to happen, and quite often, something did. While we were waiting, one of the employees wearing an elf costume stopped near Johnny and Jimmy. He was swinging a figurine on a string. Jimmy was fascinated. Then I heard the guy tell him, "Do you like this? It's a voodoo doll. It's something you can turn to when you're having problems. You can even ask it to give you power to help you."

I went into Hyper-Dad mode! I yelled, "Stop it! Get that thing away from my son!" I pulled the boys away from the guy toward Jen, and I turned back to the guy and said, "I can't believe you'd put that doll in my son's face!"

"It's just a toy," he defended himself.

"You have no idea," I insisted. "It's evil, it's wrong, and I'm not having it!"

Of course, this exchange caused quite a stir among the parents and kids around Santa Claus. A manager walked up and accused me of disrupting the situation. I told her, "You think *I'm* disrupting things? Your employee has a voodoo doll and is waving it in my son's face! It is not a child's toy. It's demonic. It has no place around children . . . or anywhere else!"

She rolled her eyes. "You'll be able to get your picture with Santa soon, so everything will be just fine."

At that moment, I took in the whole scene and realized the absurdity of me yelling about the dangers of voodoo in front of all these little children who just wanted to sit in the lap of a giant red elf with flying reindeer around him. It seemed everything in our lives had become an absurdity.

People started giving us all kinds of "helpful" advice. They told us about prayers and rituals, including how to do a salt covenant and to write verses on wooden stakes and pound them into our yard. It all amounted to what I termed "Christian witchcraft." It frustrated me that the simplicity of the gospel wasn't enough, yet we were desperate to try almost anything to help our son. The advice we heard most often was, "Have you tried playing worship music?" Yeah, we have. It doesn't really work like magic.

Triangles are simple geometric forms, but they're deadly in relation-ships. Jimmy was a master at triangulating Jen and me with himself as the ringleader. As the therapist told us, much of his acting out was directed toward Jen. Most of the time, he was sweet and obedient when I came home. Even as bad as it had been, and even though I'd seen plenty of manifesta-tions, I still wanted to "believe the best" of my little boy. I may not have said it to Jen, but when she told me about difficult days with him, my body language screamed, "It's really not that bad. You're overreacting!" You can imagine how that made her feel. Sometimes when I got home late in the afternoon, Jimmy ran up and threw his arms around me. I picked him up and gave him a big hug, but I didn't know (until later) that he had been looking over my shoulder at Jen, glaring at her and sticking out his tongue.

One day we took the kids to a local amusement fair, and JoJo won a stuffed animal. Well, it wasn't really an animal; it was a bright yellow Pokémon Pikachu (pronounced peek-a-chew). For years, I'd heard rumors that the origins of Pokémon were in the realm of the demonic, but I'd always dismissed the idea as an example of evangelical exaggeration. Now I wasn't so sure. Immediately, JoJo fell in love with it because it was yellow, her favor-ite color. It became her favorite stuffed animal. Jen and I noticed that Jimmy was fascinated with it, and from time to time, when JoJo couldn't find it and we looked everywhere she frequents, we looked in the very last place we expected to find it—in Jimmy's closet. It was impossible. We watched Jimmy like a hawk, and we didn't allow him to take anything into his room without our permission. It was very difficult to explain to an autistic child what was happening to her stuffed treasure, especially when we didn't know ourselves. Somehow, there seemed to be a strong connection between Pik-achu and Jimmy.

We had regular appointments with Dr. Amanda at the counseling center, and we enlisted everyone we knew to pray against the power of the enemy. I made a sweep of our entire house to get rid of anything and everything that might give the devil an opening. I kept only Christian music, with the exception of U2 and Creed, because those groups are "somewhat" Christian and, of course, I'm a middle-aged white guy. I went through all our DVDs and decided to implement the Kirk Cameron Rule: if the movie doesn't have Kirk Cameron, it gets thrown out. Needless to say, we watched a lot of *Fireproof* for the next few months. I found mementos I'd bought or been given when I went on mission trips to distant countries. I had kept them to remind me of how the Lord had worked there, but now, if I wasn't sure they came from the hand of a believer, they were gone.

Jimmy's fascination with JoJo's Pikachu was more than a little alarming. It was enough of a red flag for me to have a talk with JoJo to explain that the creature had to leave our home. She took it pretty well. Pikachu was the last to go into the trashcan. I poured anointing oil over the trashcan and asked God to break any curses associated with anything I threw out.

(I know . . . I can hear some of you saying, "This sounds more like paranoia than spiritual warfare. Joe and Jen were overreacting." That's what I would have concluded too before we went through this dark hole with Jimmy.)

In hindsight, I should have burned all the stuff, because a week later, the unthinkable happened. Our family was getting ready for the day. As you've probably noticed, some truck drivers tie a teddy bear or another stuffed animal on the front grill of their trucks for good luck (or to look cool or some other reason). JoJo looked out the front window and exclaimed, "There's my Pikachu!" I turned to look, and I saw her bright yellow stuffed animal tied to the front of the garbage truck. I had thrown it out in the trash a week before, and there it was, taunting us, "I'm still here!"

I felt stunned . . . and challenged. I shook my head and muttered to myself, *Damn you, Pikachu!*

The weirdness in our home never stopped. Things fell over with no one touching them, and we found tacks and nails in Jimmy's room after I'd carefully put all sharp objects in the basement. The siege attack by the enemy was relentless. Spiritual conflict buzzed in the air all day every day, even when we didn't see any visual manifestation in Jimmy.

We continued to have bizarre conversations with Jimmy when he told us that his red-eyed friends came to him and told him things they knew about us. But the strangeness wasn't limited to our home. At church he would sit in the front row with Jen and me until I got up to preach because we didn't allow him to go to children's church. One Sunday as the worship team started their first set, I looked over at Jimmy. He was manifesting, trying to yank Jen's earring out. I reached over to stop him, and like a fierce German shepherd, he bit my wrist—the wrist I'd broken years before. It hurt so bad that I dropped to my knees in front of the seats. He wouldn't let go, so I had to pry his mouth open to get my wrist out. I was sure I'd see blood gushing from the bite wound, but his teeth had bored into scar tissue, so there was no blood. The people on the worship team had a clear view of what was happening, and they were traumatized. They couldn't take their eyes off Jimmy and me—and it looked like their eyes might pop out of their heads! You can't imagine the intensity of the scene. When Jimmy manifested, it was exponentially louder than a child shouting or screaming. And it wasn't just the volume. The entire atmosphere of the room shook. You could feel the darkness. It was a shock to your system.

I'm sure the people beyond the second or third row of the congregation didn't see a thing until I picked Jimmy up and carried him with his face forward so he couldn't bite me. Then they could see me carrying my child to the back of the church, chomping at the air as he tried to get his teeth into me. I called some of our elders and a few members of our church from Africa who know how to pray down the demonic, and they gathered around Jimmy and me to pray for him. I had to rush back to lead the service. When I got up to preach a few minutes later, I was, as you can imagine, a bit preoccupied with my son's vicious behavior. I began, "People, you know me. You know I don't try to over-spiritualize or blame a demon for every problem, but I want to let you know that there's an individual in the church right now who is under the influence of demonic powers. Some leaders are in the back praying for this person. I want you to know that I'm not making this up, and I'm not exaggerating." I felt led to challenge the people: "There is a very real spiritual conflict going on all around us. If you're not right with God, if you're dabbling with a spirit of darkness, if you're denying or excusing sin in your life, you need to come forward right now and do business with God." Twenty-six people immediately got up and came to the altar to kneel and pray. We prayed over them and for them. Their response of repentance was another blessing that came from our heartache.

People all across the country and around the world were praying for Jimmy and our family. I was amazed at the outpouring of support. North Heights Lutheran Church was a very large, charismatic, Spirit-filled church in the Twin Cities. Pastor Morris Vaagenes was the retired pastor of the church and in his mid-80s. He was one of the founders of the Charismatic Movement, which includes about twenty million people from virtually every denomination. Some friends of ours attend that church, and they asked Pastor Vaagenes if he would be willing to pray for Jimmy. Our friends explained that he had been involved extensively in missions, and he had experience in praying for people who are bound by the enemy. They asked if we wanted to take Jimmy to see him. "Absolutely!" we replied.

Jen and I took Jimmy to meet with Pastor Vaagenes, and he invited the campus pastor to join us. We talked for a few minutes to get acquainted and share a little of our story, and then the campus pastor said, "Before we begin, would you mind if we take communion?"

I answered, "That would be great."

The campus pastor brought out the elements and put them on the table in front of us. He handed out the bread and then the cup, explaining that Christ is present "in, with, and under" the elements. When I took a sip, I instantly realized this wasn't an Assemblies of God communion—it was real wine! I thought, *You've got to be kidding me! I haven't had a drop of alcohol for seventeen years.* It really messed with my mind for a moment. Jen's eyes darted to mine as she took a sip. Spiritual warfare showed up where I least expected it. My mind raced: *Did this sip of wine void my sobriety date? Will I go off the rails now?* It can happen. When an innocent mistake happens and a recovering alcoholic takes even a single sip, it can throw the person off balance and start a chain reaction . . . in the wrong direction. It was as if the enemy was mocking me to my face . . . while I'm just trying to take communion.

After communion, we prayed, and Pastor Vaagenes gave us some advice. He recommended that we buy a few crucifixes, the crosses with Jesus hanging on them, and put them on the walls in our kids' bedrooms. He said, "Demons don't like people to see Jesus dying on the cross to pay for their sins."

He then asked, "Has Jimmy been baptized?"

I explained, "We're Assemblies of God, so we don't do infant baptisms. Four years old is too young."

He responded, "The symbolism and meaning of baptism sends a powerful message to demons that they don't own the person any longer. I recommend that you have him baptized."

I told him, "Okay, we'll think about it."

The two pastors, Jen, and I prayed for Jimmy's release from the forces of darkness, but as we prayed, there was no manifestation. It seemed nothing had happened as the result of fervent, believing prayer . . . again. I was very disappointed. When we finished, Jen took Jimmy to the bathroom. The pastors and I sat in the vast expanse of this huge, historic church. Pastor Vaagenes told me that it's common for demons to manifest at times like this, but since Jimmy didn't, we should just keep praying. He also said he had a sense of a serpent demon in Jimmy. Suddenly, we heard Jen scream from the lobby! Jimmy was manifesting, trying to scratch and bite Jen as she held him at arm's length as best she could.

We ran to the lobby. One of the pastors exclaimed, "I see it now!" Jimmy stopped trying to bite Jen. Now he slithered like a snake, with his tongue going in and out, sliding on the floor of the center aisle of the church. He was chomping his teeth together, loudly biting at the air. Pastor Vaagenes was walking alongside Jimmy as he slithered down the aisle, and I was walking behind Pastor Vaagenes, trying to keep him from falling down or getting bitten. It was quite the scene. Both pastors tried to lay hands on him as they prayed. Before long, Jimmy had traversed the length of the church and was at the front.

Pastor Vaagenes looked at Jen and me and asked, "Do you want to baptize him right now?"

I said, "Get the water!"

The campus pastor left for a minute or two and then returned with the water. He sprinkled Jimmy's head and again prayed for him. There was no manifestation at this point, but there was no release either. We were glad they witnessed what Jen and I had described to them. Both pastors promised to keep praying for us.

We'd been away from our other kids for four hours. We had leaned on my parents to stay with them more times than I can count during this ordeal, and thankfully, they said they were glad to help. On the way home, we stopped by a Catholic bookstore. I went in and told the clerk, "I'd like to buy five crucifixes." I figured we'd put one in each bedroom. Why not? If it's worth doing, it's worth overdoing. That's my motto!

He smiled and said, "Oh, are these graduation presents?"

I told him, "Kind of."

I'm pretty sure I could have gotten a clergy discount, but I didn't want to tell him that I'm a pastor. I was afraid he'd ask me to tell him my story, and that would take far too long.

Jen and I were exhausted, but strangely, Jimmy always seemed completely unfazed by days like this. It was about three o'clock in the afternoon, and we'd missed lunch. We were famished! We decided to stop at a Dairy Queen for a late lunch. I tried to make a joke: "For a day filled with hellfire and brimstone, there's nothing better than 'Hot Eats—Cool Treats'!" Jen gave a courtesy laugh. It wasn't my best joke ever, but it wasn't my worst either, especially given the circumstances. We ordered some hamburgers and ice cream, and we sat to eat our food. Jen and I looked at each other and we didn't have to say a word. We were both thinking, *What in the world are we going to do now?*

Two women walked in, placed their order, and sat at the table next to us, which was very awkward because we were the only people in the restaurant. I sensed there was something off with them spiritually . . . like there was a "disturbance in the force." They had weird smiles, like they were up to something. One of them pulled out her phone and started playing music. It was the theme from *The Exorcist*. I told Jen, "Let's go!"

She asked, "What's the hurry? We haven't eaten yet."

I didn't take time to explain. I just repeated, "Let's go. We need to get out of here!"

We strapped Jimmy in his seat in the back of the car, and Jen and I settled in the front. We didn't know whether to laugh or cry. I told her, "What am I going to say if somebody asks, 'So, Pastor Joe, how was your day?' I'd say, 'Well, it was a little weird: we met with two Lutheran pastors, one of whom had helped to launch a charismatic renewal movement. When we took communion, I tasted alcohol for the first time in years. Our son manifested demonic powers as a snake, slithered down the aisle of a church, and we had him baptized. I bought a handful of Catholic crucifixes, and then, when we tried to get something to eat at Dairy Queen, two women played the theme for *The Exorcist* next to us. Just a typical Tuesday. And how was *your* day?'"

At our next appointment with Dr. Amanda at the counseling center, we told her about our experience with the Lutheran pastors. She appeared to be more concerned than ever, and she told us, "I have an idea you might want to try. I have a contact with one Catholic priest, Father Luke, who is authorized to do exorcisms in this region. They don't want people to call them without references, so they require a psychologist like me to complete an assessment for the referral. It's *very* difficult to get in to see him. I'll need to be with you for the first session, and there will be a nurse and six other people who play a part, in addition to Father Luke and his assistant." She paused to let all this sink in, and then she asked, "Do you want me to make the connection for you?"

We were hesitant. This was so far out of my evangelical box. Never in a million years had I thought I would be trying to contact a Catholic priest for an exorcism. But we were desperate. "Yes, please," Jen and I said in unison.

Dr. Amanda made the call and the referral, and she set up the first appointment. It was December 2014. We were told to go to the parsonage next to a Catholic church, but Dr. Amanda asked us not to share the location with anyone else because they don't want people just showing up. As Dr. Amanda had explained to us, when Jen and I walked in, she was there with Father Luke, a nurse, six men who were leaders in the church and had assisted the priest many times before, and a lady named Sharon, who seemed to be the priest's right-hand assistant. She wasn't a nun, but she obviously served faithfully in this capacity. Before long, I realized she was the most tuned-in, wise, Spirit-filled person I'd ever met. She had such a sweet spirit combined with the gift of offering prophetic words at just the right time. Though we were all in the room, she and the priest had private communication. She sometimes wrote something on a piece of paper and showed it to him. Time after time, her input shifted the direction of the gathering. I was really glad she was on the team.

Before we began, Sharon explained what was going to happen: Jimmy would lie down on a padded therapy table with three men on each side. A sheet would be placed over his body to prevent any violent reactions hurting anyone. The rest of us stood apart from the priest, Sharon, and the men. They prayed for about an hour, and when they finished, Father Luke looked at me and said, "Dad, would you talk with me in the kitchen?"

Father Luke motioned for Sharon to join us. When we stepped into the kitchen, she put her hand on my shoulder and said softly, "I'm so sorry."

He looked heartbroken as he told me, "Yes, it's really, really bad."

I thought he might have said, "Well, Pastor, we didn't see any manifestations, so we can't help you." But that's not what he told me. He explained, "Weak demons react more quickly and overtly. Strong demons bide their time as they resist. We're not just dealing with a strong demon. I suspect we're dealing with a principality."

I must have looked like I was going to faint because he waited a few seconds before he continued. "I want to be honest with you. This kind of exorcism takes a long time, and even then, there's no guarantee that we can cast it out. The only hope is for Jimmy to be fully engaged in *wanting* to be freed from the demon."

The expression on Sharon's face told me she was deeply grieved. She softly told me, "As we prayed, I saw evil faces, demonic faces, a lot of them."

Because Dr. Amanda had recommended Father Luke and his team, and because I was convinced they were honest and honorable people who were serving God with all their hearts, I didn't resist their dismal analysis of Jimmy's condition.

Father Luke suggested we bring Jimmy once a month for the foreseeable future. I mumbled, "Okay, thanks," but I really wished we could take him every day, or at least every week. I asked him how much I owed him and the others for this meeting, and he shook his head. He told me, "Pastor, we don't take anything for what we do. It's a service to God and a ministry to people in need."

For the next thirteen months (that's right, thirteen months straight), I took Jimmy to meet with Father Luke and his team. Sometimes Jen was able to come with us, but she often had to take care of the other kids. The conversations between Jen and me were surreal, but surreal was the new normal. We'd say, "Okay, today JoJo has speech therapy, Joey has football practice, Jada goes to swimming, Johnny to wrestling, and Jimmy has an exorcism at seven tonight." Welcome to our world.

The strange events kept occurring. One night as I prayed for Jimmy, he looked at me and growled, "I'm going to wreck your blue truck." The next night, the wind blew a big limb out of a tree, and it crashed into my blue Suburban. Around the house, things continued to break for seemingly no reason, and we had recurring electrical problems. Our alarm system sometimes went off in the middle of the night, but when we checked, no one had tried to break in. The really odd thing is that we'd cancelled the service two years earlier. The fire department showed up a couple of times when the alarm didn't go off and we hadn't called them. And after they got there, they couldn't figure out how it had come on. Our car had electrical problems that mechanics couldn't figure out.

I saw things in my own home that I would never have believed could happen—there or anywhere else. One time I was standing in the kitchen late at night praying for a breakthrough, and as I was looking at the counter, a full water bottle tipped over, rolled across the counter, and fell to the ground in front of me, all "on its own." It's important to understand this about me. I've been in a Spirit-filled church my whole life, but always very conservative. I've never been into the fringe sensationalism I've heard stories about. Also, I was a bill collector for ten years, which meant I listened to people lie to me all day every day for years, plus I was trained as a cop in the Air Force. On top of that, I was an alcoholic, so I can be very skeptical and spot a phony or a lie better than most. (It takes one to know one.) Plus, I absolutely hate being tricked. I can poke holes in a lot of stories people have told me with the utmost sincerity. So I understand what some of you might be thinking: You're skeptical. I get it. I would be too. That's why I'm only relating events I've witnessed that have no other reasonable explanation. I'm not sharing the countless stories of other strange things that I didn't see with my own eyes.

By the time Jimmy was five, he was supposed to start kindergarten. The school wouldn't accept him in their regular classes, so they put him in a class for kids with behavioral issues. When we met the teacher, she looked at Jen and me like she had something on us—if our child had problems behaving, it was obviously our fault. We explained that Jimmy had been adopted from an orphanage in Haiti, and she responded, "You knew you'd have problems adopting a child from a third-world country, didn't you?" She was sure Jen and I were the problem. I'm pretty sure she assumed we'd taken on more than we could handle in adopting a child. Then, one day in class Jimmy screamed in his other-worldly voice, and it terrified the teacher. She called and asked us to meet with her, and when we walked in, she looked like she'd seen a ghost. She had encountered the darkness. From then on, she didn't minimize our perceptions . . . or blame us.

Jimmy acted out a few more times in school. He reached his limit of disruption to the class, so the principal and the teacher called to inform us that he was no longer welcome to attend. We called a county official to ask for help. After County Social Services spent some time with us and with Jimmy, one of them told us, "Children with RAD often react much more negatively to moms than dads. We recommend that we put Jimmy in a foster home with two men."

Under my breath, I asked Jen, "Is putting him with a guy or two really our best option?" I couldn't imagine it, but we were running out of ideas. I felt like we were losing any sense of control over the situation.

We continued to meet with Dr. Amanda at the counseling center. She was well aware of the complexity of our struggles and our many failed attempts to help Jimmy. When we met with her after hearing the recommendation of the CSS case workers, she told us, "In my twenty-five years of working with troubled kids, I've never seen a case as bad as this." She then said, "And I've never seen a family put so much heart and effort into finding help for their child. You have gone way over what any other family has ever done. I'm amazed at your dedication."

I'm sure Dr. Amanda meant that as a compliment, but we received it in the context of abject hopelessness.

She had come to a conclusion: "Joe and Jen, there comes a time when a situation like this destroys a marriage and a family. The two of you have done everything—absolutely everything—and now it's time to look for other options. I know of an organization that handles reverse adoptions to send kids to another family."

I looked at Jen. She was nodding that she understood and agreed with Dr. Amanda's assessment. With calm resolve, I told her, "Over my dead body. He's my son, and there's no way I'd give him up. I'd rather die than let that happen. Jimmy's not leaving our family."

Jen started crying. She was done. Remember: I'm Joe Anderson, the kid who never knew when to quit—that can be a strength or a weakness—but I'm also immensely hopeful. God had done wonders to heal the rift in our marriage, to get me sober, and to give us our children. His hand was all over me and the people I loved, and I wasn't about to give up on Jimmy. That's my heart, that's my experience, and that's my message from the pulpit: "Nothing is too difficult for the Lord!"

It took a while, but I began to see the damage that had been inflicted on Jen and the other kids. They lived in a constant state of anxiety, not knowing when Jimmy would manifest, and not knowing if they'd be the target of his violence. They had learned not to trust the times when he seemed completely normal because a traumatic event was always right around the corner. I'd been so preoccupied with Jimmy that I hadn't been as present with any of them as I needed to be. I didn't see any other option for all those months and years because our son desperately needed me, but my almost complete focus on Jimmy had come at a cost . . . to everyone.

For six months, I fought it. I couldn't bring myself to do the unimaginable. I talked to some close friends who had been supporting us in prayer for a long, long time, and I told them, "I feel like I'm dangling on the edge of a roof on a tall building. In one hand, I'm clinging to Jen and the four kids so they don't fall. And in the other hand, I'm holding on to Jimmy. I can't hold on to both of them. I have to make a decision. Either I lose my son, or I lose the rest of my family. That's my choice." Inherent in all these conversations was the nagging question that surfaced in every trial and trauma since the night of the shooting: "Why, God? Why did You let this happen to us?" Each of the trials had been gut-wrenching, but this was the worst. Hadn't we done all we could do? We took Jimmy to the Mayo Clinic, then to a retreat where godly pastors prayed for deliverance, then to the attachment counseling center (one of the best in the country), then to two Lutheran charismatic pastors, and then to a Catholic exorcist. We also had every known deliverance ministry involved in some way, along with missionaries from every part of the world praying specifically for Jimmy. Why hadn't we seen the victory?

I talked to Pastor Clarence and told him, "I don't know how much longer I can preach about the love and power of God when I'm not seeing God come through with His love and power in my own life and my family. There's an old saying, 'Are you smoking what you're selling?' How can I talk about hope and victory when it's not real in my experience? I want to be honest. I want to live with integrity. That's why I'm telling you about my deepest struggles. I need you to know what's going on with me. I just don't know how long I can keep this up."

He was very supportive. He encouraged me that God was still using me in my weakness and that there can be a power and blessing when we're "leading while we're bleeding." But on the other hand, much of the advice Jen and I received throughout this ordeal was more like magic than godly wisdom. I'm sure those people were trying to help, but many of them showed how little they understood our situation by their questions and advice. Some asked, "Have you prayed for Jimmy? I mean, *really* prayed?" Others asked if he was "just going through a phase" in normal development. Many just shrugged and muttered, "I'll pray for you, brother." A few people, thank God, saw their role as "the ministry of presence." They cared for us just by being there with us and for us throughout the struggles. They listened well, and they seldom offered any advice. Their friendship is a treasure to Jen and me.

In January 2016, I went on a twenty-eight-day fast to draw closer to God and learn more about binding the enemy in prayer. The church generously gave me paid time off for six weeks so I could focus on our family drama. I needed that time with the Lord so He could give me the courage to do the hardest thing I've ever done.

As I prayed, I imagined myself holding Jimmy in one hand and the rest of my family in the other, God gave me the grace to make a decision. I called the attorney Dr. Amanda recommended, and we began the process. The retainer was $5000. We had trouble coming up with the money because we'd spent a fortune on doctors and counselors over the years. The attorney cost a lot of money. Please don't misunderstand: I'm not complaining about any of the professionals who cared for Jimmy and the rest of us. They were generous and gracious, but their fees stretched a pastor's salary to and beyond the breaking point. The irony, of course, is that we'd paid thousands of dollars to adopt Johnny and Jimmy, and now we were paying thousands to un-adopt Jimmy. I would have given every penny I've ever made and ever will make to see him set free.

Again, Dr. Amanda made the connection for us with an organization to place Jimmy. We were asked to fill out the paperwork to inform prospective parents about Jimmy's behavior. They told us to avoid making any spiritual assessment of the cause of the behavior (like demons!), and simply describe the behavior: screaming, breaking things, biting, and so on.

Jen and I learned that the success rate of re-adopting a child is about eighty percent for kids who have psychological problems. It's attractive to families because it's free for them, and they have a very good chance of the problems subsiding to a marked extent. Before long, a couple in another state expressed interest in Jimmy; they had two other children.

It was February 2016.

The couple drove to the Twin Cities to meet Jimmy and spend a day with him. Jimmy was the perfect child—so sweet, so smart, so attentive, so responsive. We hadn't told him that we were looking for another home for him, and we didn't tell him why the couple had come to visit. Dr. Amanda had advised Jen and me not to tell him any sooner than was necessary because it would only prolong any negative reaction. As we talked, the couple told us they're Christians, but I don't think they'd had any experience with spiritual warfare.

My mind was racing and my heart was churning. I didn't want to lose my son, and I'd told my other three adopted children that they were mine and nothing would ever change that. How would they feel when they saw me hand Jimmy to another mom and dad? Joey was in middle school. I decided to fill him in on the decision and the process of un-adopting Jimmy. I also wanted to feel him out about any insecurity and doubt about his own standing in the family if we let Jimmy leave. He smiled and shook his head and said, "No problem. We're good, Dad." That was a relief. Then he said, "Dad, I have to tell you . . . I'm afraid Jimmy will kill us all someday. I'm *glad* he's leaving."

On the day the couple came to introduce themselves to Jimmy, I found some time for the two of us to be alone. I wanted to try one last-ditch effort to redeem the situation. I asked, "Jimmy, do your friends with red eyes still come to visit you?"

He replied, "Yeah."

"You know they're bad for you, don't you?" He didn't really answer, so I asked, "You know that you can be free of them if you choose Jesus."

At that point, he was getting frustrated with me. He moaned, "I know!"

I didn't quit: "Jimmy, if you ask Jesus to be your Savior and the Lord of your life, He'll set you free from your friends." He'd heard the gospel a million times, but maybe, just maybe, it would sink in this time. "If you want that, we can pray right now, and the bad spirits will have to leave. Is that what you want?"

He answered simply, "No, I don't want that."

This was the moment when I came full circle. This was the moment that I realized I could do absolutely everything in my power to help Jimmy, but I didn't have the power to change his will. He didn't want Jesus. He preferred the demons over Him. The gospel of grace is simple enough for a child to understand and accept, and a child has the free will to accept Jesus or reject Him. Jimmy said, "No." I couldn't force him to trust in Jesus.

Jimmy's decision set me free from the doubt, shame, and guilt that had been building in my heart. That night, I went into his room and told him, "Son, you're going to a new home tomorrow with the nice couple you met today."

He cried, "I don't want to!"

I wept as I told him, "I don't want you to, either, but this is what God has for you."

The next day, I took Jimmy and his suitcase to the lobby of the hotel where the couple had been staying. When we met, the man said, "Why don't we get on some Zoom calls so you can see how Jimmy is doing and he can stay in touch with you." He must have thought we were giving him away like he was one too many puppies in a litter.

I told him, "I appreciate the offer, but this is really hard on Jen and me. I think it's best that we have no contact from now on. And besides, as you attach with him, you're probably going to feel some resentment toward Jen and me. I get it. It's completely normal. For you to attach with Jimmy, Jen and I need to be out of the picture." He may have thought I was cruel or unfeeling, but I couldn't help that. We needed to make a clean break for Jimmy's sake and for us to have a chance to heal. I gave Jimmy a big hug and told him that I would always love him. I walked out of the hotel lobby and got in my car.

It was a freezing cold February morning. On the way home, I parked behind a Taco Bell because my windshield was dirty and I needed to refill my washer fluid. I was crying, and I needed some time by myself before going home. I felt a pain I've never felt before. As the reality of what just happened sank in, it felt as though a long needle was being pushed into my chest. As it passed through each layer going deeper into my chest and then my heart, the pain pierced the very backside of my heart—a place that had never been touched before. I felt violated. I was suffering from an ending that felt so wrong, so hopeless. Man, it hurt so bad. And I felt so alone. It was like a tragic death, but with no funeral, no family, no friends. I had no idea how to resolve the pain, and I couldn't think of anything anyone could do for me.

I stared at the overfilled dumpster next to the brick wall behind the Taco Bell, and when I looked up, I saw how sunny and clear the day was. That kind of crystal-clear blue sky can only happen when it's freezing cold. But my windshield was filthy from the road salt. I thought about what Paul wrote, "For now we see through a glass, darkly; but then face to face: now I know in part; but then shall I know even as also I am known" (1 Corinthians 13:12).

All the dashed hopes and dreams crushed me. It was the hardest day of my life—even harder than the morning after Jen's dad was shot, harder than Jen walking out the door, harder than any day in rehab, and harder than all the deep disappointments of unanswered prayer since we picked up Jimmy and Johnny from the orphanage in Haiti.

But as hard as that day was on me, the months and years Jen and the other kids endured may have been much harder. Day after day, Jen had suffered the screaming, kicking, lies, biting, manipulation, and confusion. And the other kids never knew if their brother was going to play with them or hurt them. His presence unsettled all of them every day, and many days he traumatized them. It was easier for Jen and the kids than it was for me to see Jimmy leave, because they had sensed the need to cut ties and protect themselves months ago.

Jen's perception about Jimmy was way ahead of mine. She had prayed just as much and just as fervently as I did, but she had come to the conclusion that it was him or the rest of us a year before I came to the same realization. She saw how Jimmy's disruption was affecting our marriage and how it was scarring the other kids. She was amazingly patient with me, her stubborn husband whose delays brought her even more heartache.

In one of our sessions with the team of exorcists, Father Luke and Sharon told us that every demon is on a mission. They each have a specific job to do, and they believed the mission of Jimmy's demon was to destroy our marriage. Mostly thanks to Jen, that mission was thwarted. They weren't alone in their assessment. Every person we met who is experienced in exorcism and deliverance ministries said the same thing: the demon in Jimmy was sent to destroy the love between Jen and me.

In the middle of our monthly exorcisms with Father Luke and his team, we scheduled a play therapy session for Jimmy while Jen and I met with Dr. Amanda. In the middle of our session, the play therapist knocked hard on our door. She came in like she had seen a ghost. Before we could ask what had happened, she told us: Jimmy had been playing with "little people" toys and acted out an entire scene of him killing our dog, Jen, and the other kids. He cut off Joey's head while Jen was on the phone with the police. She couldn't stop him. She slipped on the blood, and Jimmy killed her. He cut up the entire family and then danced around their bodies in celebration. The therapist had over twenty thousand hours of experience. She told us, "In my twenty-five years, I've never seen anything like this." She asked if we let him watch horror movies, and we explained that we only let him watch Veggie Tales. When Jimmy's therapist left the room, Dr. Amanda told us that the play therapist wasn't a believer, so she was reacting to something that didn't make any sense to her—something demonic.

That was the moment everything shifted for Jen. She went into protective mode for our family. From then on, she was on a mission to save our kids and us from the evil in our home.

I'm not sure how close we came to Jimmy's scene becoming a reality, but at one point, I thought about getting an apartment for him and me to provide Jen and the other kids some sense of normalcy, at least for a while. I decided against it. One of the people we grew to trust told us that the dark powers often try to separate a couple so they drift away from each other. Their strategy is "divide and conquer." If I'd rented the apartment, that could have happened to us. Who knows?

We don't know how Jimmy related to the couple after he left our family. We didn't hear anything about him manifesting, but we just don't have any reports. Before the couple came to get Jimmy, we asked Dr. Amanda and Sharon how they thought Jimmy would fare, and they told us that if the demon's mission was to destroy our marriage, it might lay low in the new situation. It's a theory, an assumption, but we have no information. We still pray for Jimmy every day.

I'm always very interested in how things work. I'm eternally inquisitive and love to ask questions. In another life, I'd be an investigator or an attorney. As we spent time with Dr. Amanda, I learned a lot about the intricacies of Reactive Attachment Disorder. And as we spent hours with Father Luke and Sharon, I learned a lot about spiritual warfare, the different ways demons affect people, and the importance of persistent prayer. As heart-wrenching as this time was, we learned a lot. I felt like I was getting an advanced degree in spiritual warfare, with on-the-job training. These were lessons you can't get from reading a book.

After Jimmy left our home, I thought a lot about the passage in Mark's Gospel when Jesus came down from the mountain after being transfigured and meeting with Moses and Elijah. After one of the most stunning events in the Scriptures, Jesus stepped back into the mess of fallen and wounded humanity. He walked into a crowd where the Pharisees were arguing with the disciples. What was the argument about? It was about a man whose child desperately needed help. He came up to Jesus and said, "Teacher, I brought you my son, who is possessed by a spirit that has robbed him of speech. Whenever it seizes him, it throws him to the ground. He foams at the mouth, gnashes his teeth and becomes rigid." He then explained that he had already gone to people who were considered experts because of their training, but their attempts fell flat: "I asked your disciples to drive out the spirit, but they could not." Jesus told the man to bring his son. In the presence of Jesus, the demon manifested: "When the spirit saw Jesus, it immediately threw the boy into a convulsion. He fell to the ground and rolled around, foaming at the mouth." Jesus asked how long the boy had been suffering at the hands of the demon, and his father answered, "From childhood. It has often thrown him into fire or water to kill him. But if you can do anything, take pity on us and help us" (Mark 9:14-22).

Jen and I know exactly how the dad felt. We've known his confusion and heartache, we've suffered from shattered hopes, and we've endured years of living with a child who is under the dominion of demons. I don't blame the man for telling Jesus, "If you can do anything . . ." Been there; felt that.

Jesus seemed surprised at the dad's halting plea. He responded, "'If you can'? Everything is possible for one who believes." The dam burst in the dad's heart. He exclaimed, "I do believe; help me overcome my unbelief!" Jesus commanded the spirit to come out of the boy. "The spirit shrieked, convulsed him violently and came out. The boy looked so much like a corpse that many said, 'He's dead.' But Jesus took him by the hand and lifted him to his feet, and he stood up" (Mark 9:23-27).

I identify very much with the dad in the first part of the passage. In fact, I had always felt bad for this dad because he was in a terrible predicament. But when Jesus cast out the demon, our stories diverge. His son was set free. Mine wasn't. How should I respond to Jesus? I've learned to add another sentence to the man's desire for increased faith. I tell God, "I do believe; help me overcome my unbelief! *But no matter what, I still believe.*"

When someone you love dies of cancer, when a young adult's life runs off the rails, when a marriage is strained to the breaking point, when your career hits a roadblock, when a thousand other problems seem insurmountable, when your prayers seem to bounce off heaven's doors and you want to run from God, Jesus asks, "Where will you go?" The most faith-filled response isn't one of unbridled joy; it's one of faithful determination and tenacity: "Lord, even now, I still believe." Sooner or later, God will redeem. That's His promise.

CHAPTER 9

BACK-BREAKING WORK

The months after Jimmy left were excruciating for Jen and me. When a child dies, the family members and friends find at least a measure of closure in the funeral when their eyes are turned to God's love and His promises of eternal joy. Friends come around those who grieve to offer comfort and support.

This was different . . . very different. Only a few people knew the whole story of how much Jen and I had tried to get Jimmy the help he needed, and only they fully understood our confusion and heartache. Now, when people in our church and the community heard that we'd given up our son to another family, we could anticipate the response, whether real or imagined, without hearing a word. They were thinking, *How could they? What kind of parents are they? This is the most awful thing I've ever heard!*

Jen and I were asking ourselves the same questions and coming to the same devastating conclusions . . . at least in our dark moments. We could fall back on Dr. Amanda's assessment and recommendation, and we took comfort in Sharon's stark warnings, but it was still exceptionally painful. We felt like colossal failures—as parents, as Christians, and as leaders. Shame enveloped us like a wet blanket on a cold day. As I mentioned, Jen and I had literally been the "poster parents" for adoption, but this was a huge black mark on our record. It was hard to shake the sense that we were deeply defective.

I felt another layer of shame and guilt. I'd been so preoccupied with Jimmy for two years that I hadn't been the pastor I should have been. Now I poured myself into my work to make up for lost time and convince our people that I was back one hundred percent. I wanted to institute new programs, open another campus, and expand our facilities. The busyness, I realized much later, was a coping mechanism to distract me from the intense grief of losing a son.

Jen and I should have immediately scheduled counseling sessions with Dr. Amanda to process all that had happened and the deep, conflicting emotions we felt, but after two years of counseling, exorcisms, and prayer meetings, the last thing we wanted to do was attend more meetings.

About a year after Jimmy left, Jen and I weren't in a good place. We'd bottled up an ocean of fear, doubt, self-condemnation, and shame, and it leaked out into our relationship. The anger and hurt had to come out somewhere, sometime, with somebody, and Jen and I were easy targets for one another. We needed a counselor to help us be honest with ourselves and each other so we could become partners in the grieving process instead of adversaries.

We realized there will always be a scar in our souls because of Jimmy. It was a deep, bleeding gash for a while, but as we learned to grieve and heal, a scar formed. To be honest, it still hurts to think about him, and I'm sure it always will, but grieving and healing has prevented it from consuming and destroying us. I've had to learn that life's events and decisions aren't always black and white; I've learned to live with ambiguity. I don't know why Jen had three miscarriages, I don't know why it took so long for the adoption of the twins to go through, and I don't know why God didn't answer the prayers of so many good and godly people for Jimmy's release, but I've come to the point that I don't need to know. In the depths of Job's despair over the inexplicable losses he suffered, he told those who were accusing him of hidden sin that he still believed in God: "Though he slay me, yet will I hope in him" (Job 13:15). That's my commitment too.

Part of the reason I'd been so stubborn about not giving up on Jimmy is that my identity had become wrapped up in having a great testimony of victory—in marriage, recovery, reconciliation, and adoption. I was confident everything would work out. All I needed to do was to hang in there. Being "the overcomer" became who I was, how I wanted people to see me. So the blow of Jimmy's leaving landed especially hard on me. I later realized my identity needed a radical readjustment: I'd depended on my record as a great dad, but I had to go back to depending on Jesus' record as my Savior and Lord. I realized how much my identity had been caught up in being an adoptive dad. It can happen to any of us: We can dive into ministry, caring for people, and doing all kinds of good things, and if we're not careful, we can become a little too devoted to our activities. I had to go back to me being all about Jesus.

We were at Summit Church in St. Paul for eight years. In early 2020, Jen and I felt called to Southwest Florida. As I've talked to missionaries, many of them described a similar geographical call to a country or an ethnic group. This was similar—though in February every year, every person in Minnesota feels called to Southwest Florida! But this wasn't about warm weather and beautiful beaches. In many ways, it didn't make sense: we loved the people at Summit Church, I was an executive presbyter for the Assemblies of God, my parents lived only minutes away and were very involved in the kids' lives, and we'd developed a deep, wonderful network of friends from our college days onward.

A church in Ft. Myers called and offered me a position on their staff team. Suddenly, it was like the road from the Twin Cities to Ft. Myers was lined with green lights—the call and the opportunity paved the way. However, I was going to take a steep pay cut because I would be a campus pastor instead of a lead pastor. By this time, three of our kids were teenagers, so the move would uproot them from the familiarity of their friends, schools, and activities. On top of all that, Covid's first wave had forced lockdowns and shortages all across the country. There was a lot of uncertainty about everything in 2020. Still, we felt sure this was God's leading. Jen and I always pray that we'll be willing to answer God's call, no matter what He asks us to do. We were sure this move was our next step guided by the Lord. We were filled with faith and confidence. In October, we loaded up the truck and headed south.

We found a rental home and moved in. Things at the church were really busy because it was opening up after Covid lockdowns, so I was working full speed from Day 1. But a month after we arrived, I contracted a very bad case of Covid. I had plenty to do, yet even after my primary symptoms disappeared, I still had very little energy to give to my new role. A couple of weeks later, we discovered that the house we were renting had a terrible problem with mold. We had to find a house to purchase in just a couple weeks (which ended up being the best financial decision of our lives). After we moved, however, the rest of the family got Covid. It was a crazy first couple of months in Paradise!

Gradually, certain things came to light that were very problematic at the church. The lights turned from green to yellow . . . and then to red. The new ministry clearly wasn't what I expected, and in fact, it was a terrible fit for me and my family. No matter how I tried to make things work, they simply didn't. I couldn't see a path forward there. A little over a year after we moved to Ft. Myers, on Thanksgiving weekend 2021, I resigned. The decision was necessary, but it left us in a big financial crunch. I had no backup plan; I didn't have another job waiting for me. We'd leveraged everything to move from Minnesota to Florida, so we didn't have a six-to-twelve-month emergency fund in the bank. (Sorry, Dave Ramsey!)

God's call had been clear to move to Ft. Myers, and He was just as clear that it was time to leave the church. But I didn't have a landing zone—no job, no immediate prospects, and very little money. I was confused, but not as much as our kids. They asked, "Hey Dad, are we going to have enough money for Christmas presents?" "Hey Dad, what about the expenses of graduation in a few months?" "Hey Dad, are we moving back to Minnesota?" "Hey Dad, when will you have a new job?" "Hey Dad, what should we tell our friends?" "Hey Dad, where are we going to church this Sunday?" And that's just a representative sample of their questions I couldn't answer.

Actually, I had many of the same questions for *my* Father: "Hey Dad, did I misunderstand Your call?" "Hey Dad, how did we make a move to a church where I had to discover—the hard way—that I didn't belong?" "Hey Dad, what's next?" "Hey Dad, where will the money come from? Christmas is approaching, and my future looks like a blank wall." I asked God to lead, to provide, to give me direction, but I heard nothing from Him except "Trust Me."

Except I didn't. For the next two weeks, I didn't sleep much, and I didn't eat well. I prayed a lot at night, but I was mostly complaining to God that this wasn't fair. In AA, recovering alcoholics are taught to remember the acronym HALT, which stands for "Don't let yourself get hungry, angry, lonely, and tired"—that's when we're most vulnerable to make bad decisions. I was four for four.

I'd been up all night, and I was exhausted. Early in the morning of December 14, 2021, I decided to go to the gym to burn off some of my increasing stress and anxiety. Before I left the house, I downed a big energy drink . . . after not having eaten since the middle of the previous day. I drove to the gym and started working out. Within a few minutes, I felt like I was in a dream. My thoughts were muddled, and I seemed to be drifting along in a fog. I usually power through pain when I'm working out, but this time I knew better than to keep going. I picked up my gear and headed to the door.

It had been raining that morning, so I hadn't driven my Jeep because the top was down, and it was in the garage. I was in Jen's Honda Odyssey, one of the safest vehicles on the road. I spoke to the guy at the counter as I left the gym, and that's the last thing I remember. It's not hard, though, to reconstruct what happened next. Traffic surveillance footage shows me at a stop sign just outside the gym parking lot. I sat there about a minute, ignoring multiple opportunities to drive forward. Then, I had a stress-induced seizure. My right leg shot out and stiffened, shoving the gas pedal to the floor, and my arms gripped the steering wheel like a vise. The minivan lurched across the intersection into another parking lot, hit a curb, went airborne, and slammed into a tree. It twisted sideways on the way down and hit the side of a building, Lee County Home Healthcare Center, which was filled with nurses. I found out later that two groundskeepers were working next to the tree, but the car missed them. Thank God!

People in the building thought a bomb had exploded. A number of nurses and administrators ran out to see what had happened. The minivan was smoking, so one of them ran back inside to get a fire extinguisher. The passenger side was mashed in from hitting the tree, and the driver's side was pinned against the building. There was no way to get me out, and when they looked inside, they could tell I was in the middle of a seizure.

The fire department is only a block away, so help was there in minutes. Firemen hosed down the minivan to prevent a fire or an explosion, and then one of them used the Jaws of Life to cut the passenger door open. An EMT placed a collar around my neck, put me on a board, and pulled me out. An ambulance was standing by. I was put in the back and rushed to the hospital.

On the way to the hospital, I woke up and saw a man wearing black coveralls. He was holding my foot, and I was choking from the neck brace. I thought I'd been abducted . . . and was in the back of a van! I'd watched enough Jack Ryan, Jason Bourne, and *Terminal List*—and I always imagined something like that happening to me. (Hey, just because you're paranoid, it doesn't mean people *are not* out to get you!) I started swinging, trying to hit anyone close to me! One of the paramedics shouted, "No, no. Hold on! You've been in an accident, and you're hurt really bad. Calm down!"

I stopped trying to escape. I asked, "What happened?"

One of the paramedics told me, "You were in a wreck."

I had no memory of anything after speaking to the man at the desk on my way out of the gym. During my drinking days, I passed out fairly often, but blacking out was a new experience for me—that's when you're awake but have no memory of events. Other alcoholics told me about times when they were so drunk that they lost consciousness, but that had never happened to me. It felt really odd to have no memory of an event—especially such a dramatic one.

Suddenly, I became alarmed that I might have hit someone. I asked, "Did anybody else get hurt? Did I run into anybody?"

The paramedic shook his head, and then he looked away. He wouldn't tell me anything.

I felt a little better. At least no one else was on the way to the hospital . . . or the morgue.

The stiff collar was choking me, and I felt searing pain in many parts of my body. I raised my head a little and looked at my leg. The paramedic was holding my foot because it was at a very odd angle. My ankle was dislocated, and the pain was even worse than in other parts of my body. I told the guy, "Please put my foot back in place! It hurts so bad!" He kind of winced and shook his head. I pleaded again, "Please, I'm begging you!"

He told me, "You'll have to wait until we get to the hospital. A doctor has to do it."

"I can't wait," I begged. "Please do it now!"

He looked at the other paramedic, who nodded. He gave my foot a little judo twist and jerk, and it popped back into place. I passed out from the pain.

I woke up as I was being wheeled into the Emergency Room. A nurse started cutting off my clothes. I was wearing my brand new Lululemon shorts, and I begged her not to cut them. She looked at me like, "Dude, you've got lots bigger problems than these shorts!" A few snips, and they were gone.

At that moment, a police officer came in. He didn't beat around the bush. He asked, "Sir, we're going to run blood tests, so you might as well tell me now: were you drinking or using drugs?"

I replied, "Officer, I've been sober since April 17, 1999. I'm probably the most sober person in this room."

Everybody laughed. A couple of the nurses glanced at each other and smiled as if to say, "Yeah, he's probably right!"

Radiology took scans of every inch of me. A few minutes later, a doctor walked in. He wanted to see if I had any feeling in my legs. He used a pointed probe and tapped different parts of my legs and feet. The ankle that had been dislocated was wrapped in a bandage, so he took the wrapping off so he could test that area. I told him I could feel every jab, but he didn't believe me. He thought I was reporting feeling only because I saw him touch my skin. He asked a nurse to put a towel over my face, and he went through the drill again. Still good.

He told me, "Sir, you're very lucky. I have to be honest with you. It's really bad. Your foot is broken in two places, in addition to your ankle being dislocated. Two ribs are cracked, three vertebrae exploded, and several others are cracked . . . twelve in all, and your neck is broken in three places." He patted me on the shoulder and then said, "I'm not going to be able to help you."

What? I couldn't believe what I was hearing. He wasn't even going to try to patch me up. There are certain professions where you want a level

of confidence that's almost arro-
gance—especially when it's life and
death. I wanted a surgeon with the
swagger of a fighter pilot. This was
my own *Top Gun* moment, and
this doctor was more Rooster than
Maverick when I really needed
Maverick!

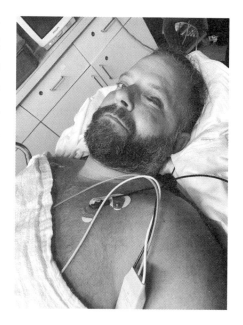

But he wasn't finished. He
continued, "I know a doctor in Ft.
Myers who is innovative. I think he
and his team can help you. I'll contact him to see if he can come right
away."

As I waited, Jen rushed into the
room. Someone from the hospital called her to tell her about the accident,
but they wouldn't tell her how badly I was hurt. She assumed the worst. She
jumped in my Jeep, with the top down, and drove in the rain to the hospital.
She wasn't sure if I was still alive. When she came into the room, I said, "Hey,
Jen. How's it going?" It wasn't the greeting she expected. She was greatly
relieved.

About two hours later, my prayers were answered and Maverick walked
in. This surgeon had the swagger of a Top Gun fighter pilot and a confident
smile that said he was up for any challenge. I was surprised when he began,
"Mr. Anderson, I want to know more about you." He sat down in a chair next
to my bed, and he said, "Tell me your story."

He had no idea how many stories I had to tell. I felt a little woozy from
the painkillers, but I launched into one story after another. About an hour
later, I noticed he was wiping tears from his eyes. "I can tell you're a man of
God," he surmised. "I'm really inspired by your life and your love for your
children. We're going to do our very best to help you recover." The doctor
scheduled surgery for the next day, and he assembled his team.

One of the great gifts from God during this entire time of surgery and physical rehab is the experience of God's presence and peace. The night and morning before the wreck, I had been deeply discouraged, critical of God, blaming Him for all that had happened. In other words, I was a wreck before the wreck. Then, in the hospital and to this day, that cloud has been blown away by a new realization of the goodness of God. In a way only He could orchestrate it, He had put another hardship in my left hand, using it to accomplish His will in my life. In my right was a powerful sense of God's presence and love, convincing me that He would never leave me.

Before long, I was wheeled into the OR. The surgeon's attention would be focused on my spine. He told Jen and me to expect the procedure to last several hours—it lasted sixteen hours. When I woke up in recovery, the doctor brought X-rays to show Jen and me what he'd done. From my pelvic bone to my shoulders, he'd rebuilt my exploded vertebrae with cadaver bones, and he'd inserted four permanent metal rods held in place by twenty-four screws through twelve of my vertebrae. He was so excited about how it had gone. He told us, "I've sent these X-rays to surgeons all over the country!"

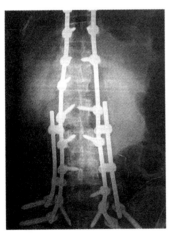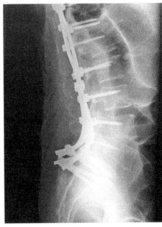

I wanted him to know that God gets the glory, so I explained, "You need to know that people all over the country have been praying for

me—and for you—today. God has answered their prayers. I'm grateful to Him . . . and to you."

I had no indication that he was a believer, but he commented, "I have to tell you, my team and I could feel it. At one point, we shifted gears. We had planned to use titanium rods in your back, but I told my assistant to get the cobalt ones because they're stronger and last longer. I told my team, 'We're using cobalt because this man is going to be active and live a long life.'"

My surgeon was speaking life over me in the OR.

The next morning after surgery, my chest really hurt. I assumed it was the broken ribs, but one of the nurses told me that when I was gripping the steering wheel during the crash, I had suffered a bilateral tear of my lower pectoral muscles. In other words, one of three chest muscles on each side had torn away from my sternum, my breastbone, and were in knots near my armpits. The nurse said this condition is very rare. I asked when they were going to fix it. This time, a doctor came to give me the news: The procedure involves surgically stretching the muscles back where they should be and screwing them to the sternum. If it was going to be done, it had to be done almost immediately after the tear happened. It was too late now. And besides, the damage to my back and neck were much more serious and required all the attention.

In my initial rehab, I was moved to a different floor in Florida Gulf Coast Hospital. The plan was to convert the floor to trauma recovery a few weeks later, but for now, I was on the floor with elderly people who had knee and hip replacements. I was by far the youngest person around. I was the first patient on the floor treated for trauma. Some of the other patients were, shall we say, a bit grumpy. They complained to the nurses about virtually everything, but God had given me a new sense of hope and optimism. The nurses liked coming in my room, and I took opportunities to share my testimony and tell them about the Lord. I prayed with them and for them. It became a place of meaningful ministry. Our family celebrated Christmas in my hospital room.

Two weeks after my initial surgery, the doctor put me on his calendar for a cervical fusion to fix my neck. His plan was to go through the front of my neck, move ligaments and vocal cords aside, and put a titanium plate and six screws in three cracked vertebrae in my neck. I wasn't familiar with this kind of operation, and I wondered how it would affect me long-term. It's one thing for a pastor to be a bit still because of back surgery, but it's quite another if he can't speak! A physician's assistant basically ran the floor. He was a strong leader, and I could tell everybody respected him. He was also a very outspoken believer. We became good friends. We're both veterans, and we shared similar views on many hot topics in the news. When he came to work every morning, he poured both of us a cup of coffee, and we sat in my room. I shared with him my fear of losing my voice, and he said that's one of the risks, but he would pray that I wouldn't lose my voice.

On the morning of the second surgery, December 30th, the nurses inserted the needle in my arm for anesthetics, and began to wheel me down the hall. My PA friend saw us and yelled, "Stop!" When he got to us, he explained, "I want to pray for my friend." While the nurses waited, he put his hands on my chest and prayed a powerful prayer: "God, I pray that the blood of Jesus would cover my brother. He's been anxious about this surgery, so I ask you for the peace that passes understanding." Then he began praying in the Spirit out loud. It was a very Pentecostal prayer. Normally, this would be a little awkward with the nurses and staff standing around us, but at a moment like that, you don't want a weak prayer like, "Now I lay me down to sleep. I pray the Lord my soul to keep." I want the power! I want a prayer of faith and promise! I'm so thankful for the gift he gave me that morning of praying for me. After that, I was fired up to go into surgery!

This surgery lasted over three hours, but it went off without a hitch. The major repairs were done. Now I needed time to heal from head to toe.

I'd been so focused on my injuries, surgeries, and recovery that I hadn't realized how the ordeal had affected Jen and the kids. Actually, it was harder on them than it was on me. At first, they wondered if I was going to live, and then they wondered how I'd be affected. Jen had been traumatized by the phone call that led her to imagine the worst. They were all wrestling with what the accident meant for our family while I was preoccupied with my recovery. But now I understood their fears.

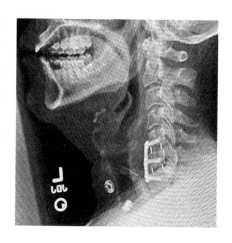

When you're hurting, there's nothing like the presence of a friend, and I had a ton of friends visit me. My lifelong friend Art VanZanten visited me all twenty-four days I was in the hospital, including Christmas and New Year's . . . that's commitment! A number of friends from Minnesota came to see me. It didn't take much to get them out of the cold in December, and it was great to see them. Rob and Becca Ketterling flew down, and they helped with some major expenses and set up an account for people to give to us. A church bookkeeper in the Twin Cities called to tell me that his pastor, a man I'd known but hadn't been close to, asked him to send us $5,000. We'd only been in Ft. Myers for a year, but people in our neighborhood spread the word about us. One had parents in New Jersey who asked their Bible study group if they wanted to help, and they sent us a check for $75. Someone started a GoFundMe campaign, and for some reason, our predicament touched a lot of hearts. Money came flowing in. Jen and I were overwhelmed by the generosity. It was one of the biggest miracles we've ever experienced. I'll never forget the kindness and compassion of so many people in our hour of need. Almost every day, Jen and I opened the mail together to read notes expressing great compassion for us, and the envelopes often included a check. We cried every day with profound gratitude.

Ironically, the first time I watched the movie *It's a Wonderful Life* was when I was spending that Christmas in the hospital. Jen had tried for years to get me to watch it, but I always found an excuse to avoid it. I was sure it was too sappy for me. Now I was a captive audience. The similarities to my

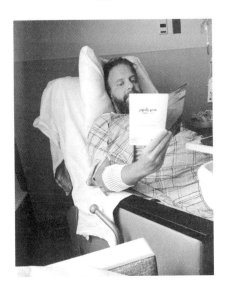

circumstances were uncanny. I cried my way through the movie, especially at the end when all the neighbors and family bring money to George Baily. I bawled my eyes out. I even had an Angel named Clarence—Pastor Clarence called or texted almost every day to let me know he was praying for me: "Remember, no man is a failure who has friends." I was the most blessed man in the world because of my friends.

In a very strange way, my time in the hospital was actually enjoyable. Yeah, I know . . . that's a weird response, and it sounds really strange . . . but it's true. I sensed God's infinite love for me, for Jen, and for our kids. I'd made new and rich friendships with the doctors, nurses, the PA, and others on the hospital staff. Like Joseph in the Egyptian prison, I was given favor and special treatment. They wheeled me outside in the sunshine for hours each day. I even had a killer tan! They seemed to enjoy taking care of me. One day when Jen was there, two of the nurses argued about how I preferred my heated blanket and my cup of vanilla ice cream just before going to sleep. Jen rolled her eyes, smiled, and asked me, "Is this what you expect when you get home?"

After a couple of weeks, now early January 2022, it was time for me to move to a rehab facility where I could receive physical therapy several times a day. Jen's sister Jodi and her husband Joe visited me to celebrate this step of progress. I told them how excited I was to start walking again. Before they rolled me out of the hospital, my home for the previous month, one of the nurses said, "We need a quick Covid test before you leave." She swabbed my nose and left to conduct the test. A few minutes later, she came back. She said, "Uh, do you want me to tell you now or after your friends leave?"

I knew what that meant. I grimaced, so she said, "Yeah, you have Covid. You're not going anywhere. We're going to have to quarantine your room until you test negative—at least ten days."

For some reason, this came as a huge blow. I started crying, and the complaints that had been so conspicuously absent suddenly appeared with a vengeance. "My chest hurts, my voice is still hoarse, my back is sore, and my foot hurts, too. This isn't a good time for me to have a deep cough!"

My friends immediately left the room. Suddenly, the only people allowed in my room wore space suits, or that's what they looked like. I had no symptoms. None. I was desperate to get out of there. I was relentless in calling everyone I could think of to get me released. I called my doctor to explain that I'd had Covid months earlier. I was very sick then, but not at all now. I asked him to pull some strings to get me out. (It felt like I was planning a prison break.) To everyone's surprise, including me, he had administrators sign papers to release me, not to the rehab facility, but home. I was only with the nurses in Martian gear for two days.

Jen picked me up, and she drove to our house. I was so glad to get out, but now Jen would have to do what the nurses had been doing to care for me. Hmmm. I hadn't thought about that. It was a tremendous amount of work, but she's a champ. She did as much as a team of nurses.

One day she wheeled me to the shower, helped me take my clothes off, and set me on a stool—which was a huge effort for her because I could barely move. She had to do just about everything for me. When she toweled me off, I got back in the wheelchair, and she gently put clean clothes on me. For some deep psychological reason, I have this thing about my socks being neatly pulled up. When she put them on, they were wrinkled and a little crooked. I looked at her, pointed at my sock and said, "Hey, you can do better than that."

Jen was wet from water from the shower and tired from being on-call 24/7. If looks could kill . . . She said only, "Do you remember what happened in the movie *Misery*?"

Instantly, I knew I'd said the wrong thing to the wrong person in the wrong way at the wrong time. I apologized profusely. "I'm sorry, Jen. I like the way you do my socks. We're good." Both of us laughed. It was a light moment that meant a lot to Jen and me. Our marriage had weathered plenty of storms, and for once, we'd gotten a laugh out of a potentially tense situation.

Jen is incredibly compassionate. I was one step away from being helpless, and she gave her best all day every day . . . with a smile. Being the recipient of her tenacious kindness has opened my eyes to couples when one cares for the other who is sick or injured, and I think I have more appreciation for all forms of kindness . . . and that's a really good thing.

Before long, I was out of the wheelchair and starting to walk again. Follow-up appointments with the doctor were very encouraging—for both the doctor and me. My recovery was way ahead of schedule. My back and neck were healing, but my foot still hurt, and sometimes it swelled. I still have residual nerve damage in my right arm down to my thumb and finger. When I continued to report that my foot still hurt, the orthopedic doctor took a longer look at it. He told me, "Your bones have healed, but you have Complex Regional Pain Syndrome. The nerves between your foot and your brain are miscommunicating, and your foot is telling your brain that your foot is still broken. That's why it still hurts and swells even though there's nothing at all wrong with it. It happens in about one in eight thousand cases." He gave me a couple of suggestions: "Walk on it like it's not broken, and put a mirror between your feet facing your good foot. Wiggle your good foot, and your brain will get the message that your bad foot is really healed. You have a brain problem, not a foot problem. This technique will, I hope, correct the miscommunication." Yeah, it sounds strange, but it fits perfectly with the rest of my life!

For over a year when I saw my surgeon and reported how well I was doing, he called me "the miracle man," which gave me the opportunity to tell him more about the Miracle Worker. I can tell that he knows God has done something special in my body.

When I went back to the gym, the people were amazed at how well I was moving. They may think it's a bit funny to see me with a mirror between my legs, but they'll get used to it.

2020 and 2021 were really hard years, but I don't regret a minute of them. I'm convinced God brought us to Florida for a reason, He led us to and from the church for a reason, and He let me survive the car crash for a reason. Through it all, I'm closer to God, Jen and I love each other more than ever, and our children are thriving. God uses everything—the good, the bad, the easy, and the hard—to get our attention, deepen our dependence on Him, and shape us a little more into Christ's image.

CHAPTER 10

SOVEREIGNTY + SURRENDER = REDEMPTION

Soon after Jen took me home from the hospital, I faced a dilemma: with all of my injuries, the doctor had put me on powerful painkillers. Through my years of sobriety, I've realized that I have very high tolerance for physical pain and a very low tolerance for emotional discomfort, which is a confusing mix for rating my pain at any given moment. Anyone who is familiar with substance addiction knows that a prescription for painkillers puts an addict in a dangerous place. The numbing felt too good. I knew that I'd never get to a point that I'd feel ready to voluntarily give up the pills, so I had to make a hard decision. I stopped taking them a couple of months before I probably should have. The pain came back in full force. Every night, I sat in a recliner. My foot was in a cast, and I wore a back brace. The cracked ribs and torn chest muscles made it painful to breathe. I hurt so bad that I rocked back and forth all night, looking for the first rays of light, which was a sign that I'd made it through one more dark time. Over and over, I prayed, "This too shall pass. God, give me strength."

As you recall, the wreck and my recovery happened after I left my role at the church in Florida. It was a time of great uncertainty, coupled with being incapacitated with mounting medical bills. I was doing physical rehab at home for months. Finally, we felt God's leading to move back to Minnesota, so we planned to sell our house as soon as possible.

In the middle of September 2022, meteorologists began tracking a tropical disturbance that could develop into a more significant depression, and perhaps even a hurricane. As the days passed, the "cone of uncertainty" began to narrow—increasingly it focused on southwest Florida, right over Ft. Myers. We were in the center of the bull's-eye! Hurricane Ian continued to grow into a Category 5 storm. When it hit, it may have dropped to a Cat 4, but when the winds are that strong, I'm not sure anyone on the ground can tell the difference. Ian made a direct hit on Ft. Myers and the eye came directly over our house. It was the most destructive hurricane to ever come ashore in that area. That's not exactly what you're looking for when you plan to put your house on the market!

In an act of God's great grace, our house suffered only minor damage. We sold our house only a couple of months later at a very good price—in fact, the highest selling price of any house in our community. Again, we'd been incredibly unlucky with the timing of the hurricane, but fortunate to get such a great price for our house. On the day of the closing, January 31, 2023, I dropped Jen and the kids at the airport for their flight to Minneapolis. I was going to drive our car back by myself. That day, it was 85 degrees and sunny in Ft. Myers, and it was 17 below zero in Minneapolis, a difference of 102 degrees. Who in the world would make that decision? Well, we would, because we were following God's leading.

On the three-day drive to Minnesota, I had plenty of time to reflect on what had happened in the past two years. God's revelation of His sovereign (and creative) purpose had begun the previous winter when I couldn't sleep because I wasn't taking painkillers. During those long hours every night, I had plenty of time to pray. I wanted God to do more than prevent me from being addicted to the painkillers; I wanted Him to do something deep in my heart. Passages of Scripture helped me make sense of this, and God seemed to weave them into a powerful concept.

The first part of the concept was a deeper recognition of God's *sovereignty.* I remembered passages about God's greatness and power, His sovereignty over all people, all events, and all times—including mine. Nothing surprises Him, and in fact, in His inscrutable will, He wants to use every event, good and bad, for His glory and our growth.

The Lord, the sovereign King, is good, loving, and gracious. As we surrender to follow Him wherever He leads, we write a new story of His faithfulness and our redemption. The psalmist captured this concept and gives us a command and a promise:

> Give thanks to the Lord, for he is good;
>> his love endures forever.
> Let the redeemed of the Lord tell their story—
>> those he redeemed from the hand of the foe,
> those he gathered from the lands,
>> from east and west, from north and south. (Psalm 107:1-3)

The second part is my *surrender* to God's will and His ways. I knew very well the kind of damage caused by stubbornness, defiance, and giving in again and again to the lure of the flesh. Refusal to surrender had cost me dearly early in my life, but surrender is not a one-time decision. *Continual* surrender to the lordship of Christ is the heart of the Christian life.

These two factors produce something deep, wonderful, and profound: *redemption*. We often think of redemption only as the initial payment for our sins, but it's more than that. We become the redeemed of God, the people who live with the knowledge that we were hopeless and helpless, but now we're deeply loved, completely forgiven, totally accepted children of the King.

We're all familiar with Romans 8:28, probably the second most-quoted verse in the Bible after John 3:16. Paul wrote, "And we know that in all things God works for the good of those who love him, who have been called according to his purpose." A lot of people have this written on their coffee mug to sip from when times are great, but when we're going through pain and chaos, it's a tough message to swallow. Even Jesus, as He faced arrest, torture, and execution, prayed, "My Father, if it is possible, may this cup be taken from me. Yet not as I will, but as you will" (Matthew 26:39).

If we take a few minutes to really think through the verse in Romans, we'll notice the tension between the "all things" and "for our good." How can we make sense of these seeming opposites? How can they be combined? Running from the tension does no good. We need to embrace it all: the tension of time, perspective, promise, our part, and God's part. As I sat in a recliner in the early hours after midnight, God gave me a concept, an illustration, a formula. It was the lightning strike I needed to make sense of God, my circumstances, and His plan. It looks like this:

SOVEREIGNTY + SURRENDER = REDEMPTION

It has become the truth that *lifts me* to the heights as I remember God's infinite greatness and wisdom—His sovereignty—and it *humbles me* to realize the only path to peace, love, and joy is by surrendering my heart, my will, and my life to that King.

Let me explain this equation in more detail . . .

SOVEREIGNTY

From the opening verses of Genesis to the end of Revelation, we see that God is the Creator of the vast expanse of the universe, and He rules over all the affairs of people and nations. We see that the only right response to the greatness and goodness of God is surrender. It's the relationship we're made for; it's the way life is supposed to work. But sadly, throughout those pages, we find thousands of accounts of people who resisted surrendering themselves to God and His will for them. Sin infected the first couple in the Garden, and it infects each of us today. Our built-in resistance to surrender is so strong that it's only overcome by the Holy Spirit transforming us from the inside out, opening the eyes of our hearts to see that surrender is the only reasonable response to our loving, powerful Sovereign.

Who is God? He is the Creator. He is good, wise, and faithful. He is both loving and just—at the same time. We would benefit from studying a thousand passages, but let me point to a few:

- He created everything . . . and I mean everything. Paul wrote, "For in him all things were created: things in *heaven* and on earth, visible and invisible, whether thrones or powers or rulers or authorities; all things have been created through him and for him. He is before all things, and in him all things hold together" (Colossians 1:16-17, emphasis added).

- Everything was created by Him and for Him. John's vision of our ultimate end includes this praise: "You are worthy, our Lord and God, to receive glory and honor and power, for you created all things, and by your will they were created and have their being" (Revelation 4:11)

- He created us in His image so we could have a relationship with Him. And yet He formed us out of the dust of the ground. We are fearfully and wonderfully made, knit together in our mothers' wombs. We are created to be in relationship with Him. (See Genesis 2:7 and Psalm 139:13.)

If you're reading this after you've suffered a horrific experience, I want to assure you that God is good, God loves you, and He is a holy God . . . a perfect God. His will and His ways are beyond our comprehension. Look into the sky and see what He has made—the whole universe from all of time exists by Him and through Him. His very voice called everything you see into existence, yet because of sin, we must respond in humility. We're so sinful that even our faintest act of rebellion or apathy made it necessary for Jesus to take the punishment we deserve, but He loves us so much that He was glad to do it.

But it helps to identify the things God is *not*:

- He's not just a "higher power." He's the Highest Power! Nothing and no one compares with Him. He's not one among many options— He's the only option! He knows you better than you know yourself, and He loves you more than you can possibly imagine. But He's also far wiser than we can comprehend. When we don't understand what's going on, we can be sure He does. In his letter to the Romans, Paul explained that God hasn't left us guessing: "For since the creation of the world God's invisible qualities—his eternal power and divine nature—have been clearly seen, being understood from what has been made, so that people are without excuse" (Romans 1:20).

Even the most brilliant minds of our day look deep into the observable code of creation and see a power holding things together. They recognize laws and rules to the universe given by a good Creator. This is more than intelligent design—it's God's divine, specific creation. We aren't in a simulation from some other dimension of time and space, and we're not just a cosmic accident from nothingness.

- God isn't our copilot or a genie in a bottle. He's not our waiter taking orders to make our lives more comfortable. We exist for Him: to know Him, respond to His great love for us, and serve Him with all our hearts. Yes, there are countless blessings He gives, but each one is designed to point us back to worship, gratitude, and glad obedience.

THE + SIGN

How can we relate to someone so powerful, so wise, so holy? Not by trying to impress Him by being good enough, but only by receiving His gift of grace.

The plus sign in the equation represents the cross.

We have nothing to add, no way to earn God's acceptance, no trick to manipulate Him to love us. We only look at the cross of Jesus and marvel that He paid the ultimate price for us. In fact, His last words before He died were, "It is finished," or in another translation, "Paid in full."

We aren't pretty good people who need a little grace. We're desperately lost people who need to be found. We're dead spiritually and need to be made alive. And the only one who can make this happen is Jesus. He told people, "I am the way and the truth and the life. No one comes to the Father except through me" (John 14:6).

On the morning I left Ft. Myers to drive back to Minnesota, I drove over to the gym and stopped at the tree I'd crashed into a little more than a year before. I parked near it and spent a long time thinking and praying. The tree was still standing, though it had an ugly scar. I'd left my mark. The Lord reminded me of a verse, "Christ redeemed us from the curse of the Law, having become a curse for us—for it is written: 'Cursed is everyone who hangs on a tree,'" (Galatians 3:13). I thought about our time with Jimmy. When I quoted this verse, Jimmy writhed and twisted and tried not to listen. Demons understand the meaning of the cross, and they don't want people to experience the freedom and power it brings. That told me how important this truth is—in the seen world and the unseen world.

I also thought about all the times I've felt cursed. Those were painful moments, but they don't compare with the ultimate curse of dying without Jesus. The enemy wants us to live in defeat, and the biggest defeat is death without salvation. Jesus shared the stark contrast in purposes: "The thief comes only to steal and kill and destroy; I have come that they may have life, and have it to the full" (John 10:10).

I could have died on that tree in the parking lot, but Jesus died on a tree outside the gates in Jerusalem in my place. This truth has captivated me, so I don't fear death at all. In the hospital, when the doctors and nurses told me repeatedly that it was luck that I didn't die in the wreck, I had two profound thoughts: First, my gratitude wasn't focused on being spared from death; I was thankful Christ has saved me for eternity. More than ever, I was aware of the price He paid for me so I could be a child of God, live in His kingdom now, and live with Him forever. And second, I had an overwhelming desire to share the love of Christ with everyone I could. I love them because Jesus' love for me is overflowing from my heart. All of life boiled down to those two truths: God's grace and the love of Christ. This realization changed me in profound ways. Yes, I can forget, and I can be distracted, but I have strong memories that bring me back and refresh me.

SURRENDER

The first step in recovery from an addiction is "Admit you are powerless" over the substance or behavior. The first step in walking with God is the same: to admit that we desperately need God's heart and His power. Again, I look back at the two verses in James that have become a cornerstone for me: "God opposes the proud but gives grace to the humble. . . . Humble yourselves before the Lord and he will lift you up" (James 4:6, 10).

I'm afraid a lot of people have the wrong idea about surrender. It's not sitting passively and waiting for God to do it all. Surrender is active. It's trusting God when we see no way forward. It's moving ahead in faith when we aren't sure where to go. It's spending time getting to know the heart of God, His compassion and wisdom, so that surrender becomes the only reasonable choice.

After Peter confessed Jesus as the Christ, Jesus gave His disciples marching orders: "Whoever wants to be my disciple must deny themselves and take up their cross and follow me. For whoever wants to save their life will lose it, but whoever loses their life for me will find it. What good will it be for someone to gain the whole world, yet forfeit their soul? Or what can anyone give in exchange for their soul?" (Matthew 16:24-26) In other words, choosing God's agenda, surrendering to Him and His will, always involves saying "no" to our selfish desires and saying "yes" to Jesus and His plans. At this point, many people back away because they conclude the price is too high. But the promise is that surrender opens the door to real life— living in God's presence for eternity, yes, but also experiencing His love, presence, purpose, and power now.

But the question remains: Why would I (or anyone else) willingly and even gladly surrender to God's leadership? I'm not suggesting it's easy to surrender to God, but it's simple. I've struggled with it again and again, especially during particularly difficult times. When hard times come, I naturally want *my* will to be done—I want peace, security, and above all, answers! Will I trust God in the middle of the trials? Is He enough? Again, why would anyone, including me, surrender to God's will and ways? Because of the cross. The gospel isn't just for the day we first trusted Christ; it's the powerful motivation and inner strength to walk with God all day every day.

Almost everybody who goes to church can repeat, "Jesus died for our sins," but what does that mean? First, it means that we are deeply fallen, tragically flawed, and we have no way to dig ourselves out of that hole. It took the substitutionary death of the Son of God to pay for ours sins. Some faithful church attenders depend on their ability to follow God's rules well enough so that He will say, "Okay, good enough. You can go to heaven." Trusting in our ability to follow rules is called legalism. It was the way of life for the Pharisees who were proud of their commitment to rigid, lifeless obedience. It made them surly, not surrendered.

Far too often, we're satisfied with Jesus as our Savior, but we resist following Him as our Lord. If that's the case, it shows that our concept of God is far, far too shallow. I love the vision of Jesus in John's opening of Revelation. See if this is someone you'd follow:

Then I turned to see the voice that was speaking with me. And after turning I saw seven golden lampstands; and in the middle of the lampstands I saw one like a son of man, clothed in a robe reaching to the feet, and wrapped around the chest with a golden sash. His head and His hair were white like white wool, like snow; and His eyes were like a flame of fire. His feet were like burnished bronze when it has been heated to a glow in a furnace, and His voice was like the sound of many waters. In His right hand He held seven stars, and out of His mouth came a sharp two-edged sword; and His face was like the sun shining in its strength. (Revelation 1:12-16).

When John saw this vision, he didn't turn to someone next to him and say, "Hey, there's a nice guy I can try to emulate." And he didn't say, "That's my copilot." No, this was his response: "When I saw Him, I fell at His feet like a dead man. And He placed His right hand on me, saying, 'Do not be afraid; I am the first and the last, and the living One; and I was dead, and behold, I am alive forevermore, and I have the keys of death and of Hades'" (vss. 17-18). This is the one we follow. This is the one who is worthy of our total surrender.

Surrender is the only right response to God's greatness and goodness. After eleven chapters explaining the wonders of God's saving grace, Paul tells his readers in Rome, "Therefore, I urge you, brothers and sisters, in view of God's mercy, to offer your bodies as a living sacrifice, holy and pleasing to God—this is your true and proper worship" (Romans 12:1). Salvation happens in a moment when we put our faith in Christ and are transferred from one kingdom to another, but surrender is a movement, a continuous trust in God to empower, lead, and use us in the lives of others. We're to offer our bodies as living sacrifices, but as one sharp leader said, "The problem with a living sacrifice is its tendency to crawl off the altar."

After my back and neck surgeries, my foot was still in a cast as I began rehab. Before the doctor let me go to the gym to start working out, I had to start walking. But I was a mess: My chest muscles were torn, I needed rotator cuff surgery for both shoulders, my back and neck were very tender, and my foot continued to hurt for months after it looked like it was healed.

During my first few times at the gym, I waddled around, barely able to walk without falling, and I sure hoped no one would bump into me! I began by lifting one-pound dumbbells. (I'm not sure you should call them dumbbells. They were more like the weight of a few coins.) But even lifting them was an enormous effort and left me sweating profusely. It would have been terribly embarrassing, but hey, I had a lot of excuses. Working out was real labor. If I'd waited until I felt strong before starting to work out, I would never have begun. I could have sat on the sofa all day every day watching television and eating nachos—which sounds delicious! But I was well aware of the sacrifices people had made to get me to that point: the surgeon who had inserted the cobalt rods, screws, and cadaver bone in my back and a titanium plate in my neck; the people who had mined the ore and processed it to provide the cobalt and titanium; all the other medical professionals who'd devoted years to prepare so they could help people like me; and even the person who had donated his or her body so I could have bone made into paste to rebuild the vertebrae in my back.

Now, it was my turn to do my part. I worked out, stretched, took supplements, got plenty of sleep, walked, and kept my weight down . . . and did it all again the next day, and the next. Salvation is all about Jesus. We play no part in that, except to receive His gracious offer. But spiritual growth requires both God and us. We're partners in the process of healing emotional wounds, producing the fruit of the Spirit, and making a difference in the world around us. Paul put it this way, "So then, my beloved, just as you have always obeyed, not as in my presence only, but now much more in my absence, work out your own salvation with fear and trembling; for it is God who is at work in you, both to desire and to work for *His* good pleasure" (Philippians 2:12-13, emphasis added). If I thought it was all on me and I tried to heal without having the surgeries, I would have been on the floor like a jellyfish after one step. I needed outside intervention. But I also had to do my part, and the result is amazing progress.

From all of my experiences with alcoholism, a severely strained marriage, miscarriages, autism, demonic activity, hitting a dead-end at my job, and a severe accident, I'd say that we're in a war for our souls. I'm not trying to be overly dramatic . . . just honest and accurate.

One of the most profound moments in any movie I've ever seen was in the series, *Band of Brothers*. After D-Day, Easy Company of the 101st Airborne was engaged in a series of battles in France and Belgium. Lieutenant Ronald Speirs was known for his reckless bravery. One night, Speirs came upon Private Albert Blithe who had been in a foxhole. When a noise startled Blithe, Speirs saw a teachable moment. He asked the private to tell him about his service since the landing on the beaches in France. Blithe related how scared he had been, especially while hiding in a ditch during the fierce fighting on D-Day. Speirs asked him, "You know why you hid in that ditch, Blithe?"

Almost silently, he replied, "I was scared."

Speirs told him plainly, "We're all scared. You hid in that ditch because you think there's still hope. But Blithe, the only hope you have is to accept the fact that you're already dead. And the sooner you accept that, the sooner you'll be able to function as a soldier's supposed to function. . . . All war depends upon it."[6]

That's a central message of the gospel. If we're "in Christ," we're in Him in His death, so our sins are forgiven; we're in Him in His life, so His righteousness is credited to us; and we're in Him in His resurrection, so we have new life in the Spirit. To truly live for Christ, we have to consider ourselves dead to our selfishness.

What's a grateful response to the wonder of God's grace to us? "For we are God's handiwork, created in Christ Jesus to do good works, which God prepared in advance for us to do" (Ephesians 2:10). Grace comes before doing good, but grace always leads to doing good. The order is important.

REDEMPTION

The word *redeem* used to have more meaning than it does today. In popular use, it only means to take advantage of a coupon or a gift card, but actually, it means *to buy back, to regain possession of something through a payment.* It's the perfect word to describe what Jesus did for us on the cross. The cross of Jesus is the dividing line in all of history, and it's the dividing line in the human heart. The Pharisees thought they could follow God's law closely enough that they could earn their place in His kingdom, but they forgot that breaking the law at any point brings the curse of the law upon them—and since God's law reaches even into our deepest desires and motivations, no one comes close! The Old Testament, especially Deuteronomy, outlines the requirements and the curses of the law, but because no one can keep it, the law always pointed to Someone who would keep it for us.

We can identify two types of redemption, one related to "the already," and the other to "the not yet." Let me explain.

One type (what I call "capital R" Redemption) is positional and eternal—the present, sure hope of heaven that we haven't yet experienced. For all of Christian history, and especially during dark times of suffering, believers have longed for heaven. Today, it seems many of us expect heaven on earth, and we've lost the intense desire to be with Jesus in the place where there will be no more tears or regrets. We could learn something by reading the lyrics of slaves' songs about the hope of heaven, confidence in the eternal justice of God, and this world not being our home.

On my second day as an eighteen-year-old camp counselor at Lake Geneva Bible Camp, I learned that a third-grade boy had suffered severe abuse in his home. His emotional pain came out at every meal. He had panic attacks and choked, even when he was only drinking water, and he would run out of the cafeteria. We contacted the authorities, and after an investigation, they directed that the boy be put in foster care when the week was over. The boy had suffered abuse, and now he felt abandoned and isolated. He was so afraid. An older pastor was at the camp that week, and for days after we learned about the horror of the boy's homelife, he took the boy down to the dock at mealtime to look at the tranquil beauty of the lake while they ate. I was really concerned for the boy, so I asked the pastor, "What are you telling him? How are you comforting him?"

The pastor said with great compassion and wisdom, "I'm not telling him everything will be okay. I'm not telling him that he just needs to try harder to please his parents or try harder to control his panic attacks. I'm not telling him that if he makes the soccer team, his life will be a lot easier. All of those would be lies. He's going back into a very difficult situation. When we sit together down at the dock, I tell him about heaven. I tell him there will be no suffering, no heartache, no fears, and no tears. Then and there, God will make everything right. That's the only sure hope I can give him."

Instead of telling ourselves and each other that it's God's job to make our lives easy, successful, and fun, we need to read our Bibles more carefully and realize the heroes of the faith looked far ahead for their comfort. The writer to the Hebrews lists men and women who endured hardships with faithful hearts, and concluded that they "confessed that they were strangers and exiles on earth" who were "seeking a country of their own . . . a better country, that is, a heavenly one" (Hebrews 11:13-16).

Heaven is in the future, but the cross is in the past. In the Old Testament, the writers pointed to a day when God would do for us what we can't do for ourselves. They looked forward to the cross; we have the privilege of history—we can look at it in the rearview mirror.

God gave Abraham a sweeping promise to become the father of a great nation, to be blessed and pay it forward to bless others. But he and his wife Sarah were old, and for years, the promise of a child didn't happen. He decided to shift to Plan B, naming one of his servants as the heir of the promise. In response, God took him outside and pointed to the stars. He promised, "So shall your offspring be."

To reinforce this promise, God made a solemn covenant with Abraham. In those days, two people didn't sign a contract when they made a formal agreement. They acted out the consequences of *not* following the conditions of the agreement. Always, the lesser party acted out the consequences, not the greater. God told Abraham to bring a number of large animals, cut them in two, and lay the halves so there was a path between them. And He told him to put birds on either side. I'm sure Abraham expected God to tell him to walk between the carcasses as a warning: "This is what will happen to you if you fail Me!" But that's not what happened.

As the sun set, Abraham fell into a deep sleep, "and a thick and dreadful darkness came over him." As he slept, God filled in some gaps in His promise: his descendants would be enslaved for four hundred years, but they would be freed and come back to the place where they were meeting. Then, something amazing happened: "When the sun had set and darkness had fallen, a smoking firepot with a blazing torch appeared and passed between the pieces. On that day the Lord made a covenant with Abram and said, 'To your descendants I give this land, from the Wadi of Egypt to the great river, the Euphrates.'" The smoking firepot reminds us of the fire and smoke when God met Moses on Mt. Sinai; the blazing torch is like a streak of lightning in the sky, but was constant, not a flash and then gone. Both of these are symbols of the presence of God himself! God, the far greater party in this covenant, was saying, "If I don't come through on My promise, I'll suffer the consequences . . . but if you don't come through, I'll suffer them for you." Over two thousand years later, God, in the form of Jesus of Nazareth, suffered the consequences for the failure of the children of Abraham—not just his Jewish descendants, but "all peoples on earth." This is at least one of the places where we see the gospel of grace powerfully depicted in the Old Testament (Genesis 15:1-18).

Who is the One we surrender to? It's the One who surrendered himself for us. When Jesus was in the Garden of Gethsemane before His arrest, He peered into the abyss of hell and prayed, "Let this cup pass." But if He didn't drink the cup of judgment, all of us would be doomed to suffer that judgment—eternal separation from God where "the worm does not die and the fire does not cease." When He asks us to surrender, Jesus isn't asking us to do anything He hasn't already done to the nth degree. He stepped out of the glory of heaven, surrendering to the Father's will and limiting himself for our sake. The cross assures us that heaven is coming.

But there's another type of redemption ("little r" redemption) which is situational and temporal. This type focuses on what God is doing today, right now, in our current blessings and trials. We walk with Him through the waters of healing, deliverance, sobriety, forgiving those who have hurt us, and asking for forgiveness when we've wronged people. We trust God for courage to speak the truth, even when it's uncomfortable, to love the unlovely, and to care for those who can give us nothing in return. In darkness and light, we cling to the One who knows the way.

We see this pattern in the life of Joseph, who was betrayed by his brothers, sold into slavery, falsely accused by his master's wife, and sentenced to years in an Egyptian dungeon. It all seemed so senseless and wrong. It took a long time for Joseph to realize that God's path led through dark valleys before he came out into the light, but in the end, he could tell his brothers, "As for you, you meant evil against me, but God meant it for good in order to bring about this present result, to keep many people alive" (Genesis 50:20). I'm not sure when Joseph had that aha moment that the dream God gave him when he was a boy had finally been fulfilled. He realized all the pain and loneliness was accomplishing God's divine plan, and that was enough for him. And Jesus certainly didn't live under any illusions that life would be easy. He gave the promise most of us don't want to hear, at least the first part: "In the world you have tribulation, but take courage; I have overcome the world" (John 16:33).

Centuries ago, Gregory of Nyssa said that his friend Basil had "ambidextrous faith" because he took the blessings of God in one hand and life's heartaches in the other, trusting God to use both to equip him to accomplish His will.[7] That's what my life is about. Throughout this book, I've described my journey to live with ambidextrous faith. I began with the false assumption that God wants, above all, for me to be happy, and He would orchestrate my life to be pleasant. That's what I thought it meant to be "blessed." Through all the ups and downs, I've realized that God's will and ways are much deeper, richer, and more complicated than superficial happiness. Grace means more to me than an entry into the kingdom. Grace is the power to enjoy the great things God gives, and also is the source of power to make meaning out of a mess.

This experience of God's grace gives us confidence to weather any storm. When I was in the ambulance after my wreck, I was in tremendous pain, and I knew I was badly injured. The look on the paramedics' faces told me I was in trouble, but I wasn't afraid of dying. I certainly didn't want to leave my family, but I was convinced that Jesus had me in His hands, and that was enough for me.

I think one of the clearest theologies of suffering is in Paul's second letter to the Christians in Corinth. Throughout the letter, he describes how he was near death, but God rescued him; he worried that the believers in Corinth had abandoned him, but they proved to be faithful; he cataloged a long list of trials, but God had come through each time. Then, near the end of the letter, he describes a moment when he suffered from "a thorn in the flesh." Different scholars and pastors have speculated what the "thorn" might be, but we simply don't know. Actually, I'm glad he didn't describe it because each of us can identify with some form of a thorn in our own lives, and the remedy is the same for all of us. Paul, a man of powerful faith and prayer, prayed three times that God would take it away. I think the mention of three times means Paul beat on the doors of heaven to give him relief, but he got an answer he didn't expect. God told him, "My grace is sufficient for you, for my power is made perfect in weakness." Paul then makes a sweeping application: "Therefore I will boast all the more gladly about my weaknesses, so that Christ's power may rest on me. That is why, for Christ's sake, I delight in weaknesses, in insults, in hardships, in persecutions, in difficulties. For when I am weak, then I am strong" (2 Corinthians 12:7-10).

Have you recognized the truth in this paradox? Have you had to dig deep when you were weak until Jesus gave you supernatural strength to persevere? Christians can learn a lot from people who have gone through the process of addiction recovery. They don't start getting help until they admit they're powerless, and they make progress only by continuing to admit their flaws, sins, and shortcomings, which provide a springboard for repentance. Rigorous honesty produces humility, which gives them the power to make good decisions. It's the same for each of us: when we're honest about our flaws and weaknesses, we look for a rock in the middle of the storm—and that rock is Jesus.

As strange as it may seem, I'm grateful for my alcoholism—not the sin and the damage it did to me and those I love, but the lessons I've learned from walking out of it. This weakness has driven me into the arms of God, and it has made me stronger. I've been sober since April 17, 1999, and I don't take sobriety for granted. You don't get a prize for being sober for over twenty years, but you get the blessing of being sober today. And all I have is today. One day at a time, one moment at a time, trusting Jesus to use my flaws to make me more dependent on Him and to give me compassion for others who struggle with heartaches in their lives.

If God has shined a light on your heart and you realize you need a Savior, embrace the One who gave everything to bring you home to Him. Tell God that you've sinned, and you need His forgiveness. Tell Him that you want Him to transform you from the inside out. You might pray something like this: "Lord Jesus, I need You. Thank You for dying on the cross to pay for all my sins. I accept Your sacrifice for me. You paid for it all. It's finished. Thank You for transferring me from the kingdom of darkness to Your Kingdom. I'm all Yours."

If you expressed your heart to God in this way, you can breathe a deep sigh of relief. Jesus has done for you what you could never do for yourself. Thank Him. Praise Him. And delight in His love. The moment we place our trust in Christ, God does heart surgery and changes the destination of our eternity. The apostle Paul's shorthand for those who have trusted Jesus is the brief phrase "in Christ" or "in Him." Throughout his letters, he explains that those who are "in Christ" have new hearts, ones that can respond to the love of God, are open to the leading of the Spirit, and love the people God loves, which is everybody. And our address changes: we're delivered from Satan's kingdom to God's. We get a taste of that kingdom now, but someday, we'll be with Him face to face.

To grow in your faith, find a church where the gospel is central to the message, begin reading the Gospel of John, spend some time praying every day, which is just talking to God and listening to Him, and find some new friends who will help you grow in your faith. You'll want to learn more about the God who loves you so much, and you'll want to spend time with people who are responding in faith to His sovereignty and kindness.

A second person I want to address is anyone who has suffered such trauma, such heartache, such pain that he or she is thinking of throwing in the towel. God seems absent. He's unfair. He hasn't answered prayer the way you want. I hope this book has given you a strong sense of hope—not that "everything will turn out right," but that your wise, loving, sovereign God is walking with you through your darkest days—even when you don't sense His presence. I've talked to men and women who were about to give up on their marriages. I've had many conversations with parents of wayward teenagers and adult children. Their hearts have been broken by seeing the self-imposed destruction, and they've cried out to God. I know people who have suffered the pain of losing children through miscarriage or a childhood disease or an accident. They feel shattered, and they're not sure they can ever be whole again. I've talked with people who have hit a dead-end in their careers, sat in a doctor's office and heard a devastating diagnosis, had a friend or family member betray them, or watched a parent or spouse gradually drift away in dementia. In all of these and countless other heartaches, the answer to life's problems sometimes is a glorious miracle, but more often, we need the miracle of ambidextrous faith.

Quite often, the first step is to tell someone you trust that you're struggling. Find that person—a pastor, a counselor, a close friend, or your spouse—and take the risk of being honest and vulnerable about the one thing you've most dreaded admitting! The first step will lead to others. For instance, make an appointment with your pastor or a counselor, see a doctor to get an accurate diagnosis, learn more about forgiveness and practice it, make amends, attend recovery meetings. When we trust God in the wintry seasons of our lives, people notice, and they marvel. It may be the most powerful testimony we can share with them.

Far too often, we focus on what's happening right now, but we need a long-range view. I've heard a pastor say that we don't grasp a billionth of what God is doing in us, around us, through us, and in spite of us. He is infinitely wise; we're not. We often "see through a dark glass," but God points us to the certainty of a glorious future. When we're discouraged about what's going on today, we can be sure that someday, everything will be made right—in heaven, and then in the new heavens and new earth, the renewal of all things. But our suffering today isn't the end of the story.

Paul points us to a hope that can't be taken away or diluted by our current circumstances. In fact, the pain and confusion we experience now makes us long for eternity that much more. It's like being a lifelong, tortured Minnesota Vikings fan: when they finally win the Super Bowl, the wait will make the win that much sweeter! Paul explained, "Therefore we do not lose heart. Though outwardly we are wasting away, yet inwardly we are being renewed day by day. For our light and momentary troubles are achieving for us an eternal glory that far outweighs them all. So we fix our eyes not on what is seen, but on what is unseen, since what is seen is temporary, but what is unseen is eternal" (2 Corinthians 4:16-18).

There's a third person I want to speak to: you who are passionate about a particular ministry of the church. I can't guarantee it, but I suspect that most times when we see someone who is endlessly enthusiastic about ministering in a certain area, it's because he or she has probably had experience in dealing with a related problem. People who have struggled in their marriage and have seen God turn resentment into rekindled love often are the ones who are active in marriage ministries. People whose lives have been saved from alcohol or drugs are eager to help others who are struggling with the same problem. People who work to coordinate prison ministry probably either were incarcerated themselves or had a family member in jail. Those who have climbed out of the pit of debt can't wait to share what they've learned with others who struggle with finances. Couples who tried for years but were unable to have children, and finally opted for adoption, have their hearts filled to overflowing with joy and encouragement for others considering adoption. The list goes on, but you get the picture. Redeemed pain is always a rich, life-changing story. When God has worked powerfully in our lives, we naturally want to pay it forward. Just as the great theologian Kelly Clarkson sang, "What doesn't kill you makes you stronger!"

Does your heart sing like this? I hope so, but I also know how long and hard the road has been for me to arrive at this point. Surrender requires us to give up on our demands to be in control, know everything that's happening, and guarantee an outcome. When we surrender, soon our hearts are filled with wonder that God knows, God cares, and God is working His will in His own way. That's the real source of "the peace that passes understanding."

As I look back on our family's story, I believe one moment was pivotal more than all the others. After the third miscarriage, Jen and I wanted to curl up, close out the world, and cry. We didn't want to be with anybody, we didn't want to answer any questions, and we didn't want to have people stare at us. But that Sunday morning, we decided not to isolate. We went to church. It was our statement to God that we were surrendering our hopes and dreams to Him. As we stood, cried, and sang, friends came from all around the church to stand with us, hug us, and cry with us. It meant so much. But we were also surrendering our expectations that God would give us what we wanted. We'd prayed, but He hadn't answered. We could either be resentful and back away from Him, or we could move toward Him, trusting that He knew better than we did. That morning, the blessing wasn't a child in a bassinet; the blessing was God's peace. We were echoing Jesus' prayer in the Garden, "Not my will but Yours be done." If we hadn't been open to God that morning, we almost certainly wouldn't have responded positively to the invitation to attend an adoption information meeting. God blessed—not in the way we hoped, and not in the way we expected, but in the way He chose to bless us.

I'm sure some who are reading this book identify strongly with the prophet Joel who compared the devastation of God's people to a ravaging invasion of locusts. But Joel's message to the people of God didn't end with this dire assessment. Through the prophet, God promised: "I will repay you for the years the locusts have eaten" (Joel 2:25).

Again, a sovereign, wise, almighty God is more than able to work in our lives, but He brings us low, to humble us so we'll surrender and seek Him with all our hearts. Then, we experience the wonder of redemption— not always the answer to our initial prayers, but the answer to our reshaped prayer that God would do whatever it takes for His glory and our growth.

Throughout my time in recovery, I was taught "The Serenity Prayer," written by theologian Reinhold Niebuhr during the turbulent days of World War II. Many people can recite the first few lines, but I want share the full prayer with you. I hope you'll pray it with me.

God, grant me the serenity
to accept the things I cannot change,
the courage to change the things I can,
and the wisdom to know the difference.
Living one day at a time,
enjoying one moment at a time;
accepting hardship as a pathway to peace;
taking, as Jesus did,
this sinful world as it is,
not as I would have it;

trusting that You will make all things right
if I surrender to Your will;
so that I may be reasonably happy in this life
and supremely happy with You forever in the next.
Amen.

You can always test if a message is true to the gospel if it applies the same whether you are celebrating on the top of the mountain or struggling in the lowest valley. So if I had only enough breath for a final message for you to take from this book, it's this . . .

"SERVE JESUS. SERVE JESUS. SERVE JESUS."

ENDNOTES

1   From the lyrics of "Baby" by Justin Bieber on the album *My World 2.0.*

2   "Welcome to Holland," Emily Perl Kingsley, 1987, http://www.our-kids.org/Archives/Holland.html

3   Rob Ketterling, *Fix It!* (Burnsville, MN: River Valley Resources, 2018), pp. 210-211.

4   From the television cartoon show, *Wonder Twins.*

5   For more information, see https://scholar.harvard.edu/amcgee/publications/marasa-elou-marasa-twins-and-uncanny-children-haitian-vodou

6   *Band of Brothers,* this conversation cited on imdb, https://www.imdb.com/title/tt1247463/characters/nm0786136

7   Cited by Philip Yancey in *Reaching for the Invisible God* (Grand Rapids: Zondervan, 2000), p. 69.

ACKNOWLEDGMENTS

As you can imagine, quite a number of people have poured into my life to encourage, support, and sometimes redirect me. These people mean the world to me:

JEN: Jen and I have been married for over twenty-six years, which is a long time, but our crazy experiences add up to many lifetimes of hardship and pain as well as victory and joy. Our relationship truly is a redemption story. We have a closeness like that of war buddies who have spent numerous battles in foxholes together. We get each other. We have a perpetual inside joke that could only be explained by saying to others, "You had to be there." Like a broken bone that has healed stronger than before, our relationship continues to grow. Complacency or a lukewarm love has never been an option for us. We've had to fight for our love every step of the way, but God has given us a love for each other with layers of connectedness that only come through Christ redeeming our pain. We also have never stopped laughing and joking.

JOJO: Beautiful, playful, and athletic. Even with autism, God is using her in every situation to be a magnet for people, a light of kindness and love. She doesn't waver in her faith and beliefs. She loves the Word of God and listens to the Bible every night. She's gifted with compassion and discernment.

JOEY: He has always loved the things of God and is glad to help out in any way. Ever since he could walk and talk, he has followed me to church and ministry events. He has the unique ability to bring people together and create excitement. He is physically strong and has a million-dollar smile that lights up every room, but he's also sweet and sensitive to the things of God. He's had a knack for fashion and design ever since he was a baby. He is using his gifts for a degree in marketing while serving in the local church.

JADA: She hit the genetic jackpot because she looks exactly like a tall and blonde version of Jen. She's intelligent, witty, funny, and can be as stubborn as I am. She has a quiet strength with a loving heart. Little kids always gravitate to her and look up to her. She has always had a desire to go into the medical field and use her gifts to care for people.

JOHNNY: He's handsome and charming, eternally inquisitive, and knows as much as a zookeeper about wildlife. He has experienced so much in his life, and out of darkness, he has chosen the light of Jesus Christ. His passion for God and his creativity comes through everything he does.

I couldn't be more proud of my family. We've been through a lot. It breaks my heart to think of what my kids have had to witness as kids and teenagers, but they have also seen God's faithfulness in miraculous ways.

To be honest, I really didn't want to write this book, but I know God has called me to write it. It truly is "let the redeemed of the Lord tell their story." My prayer for our family, and now for you, is a prayer I call "double for our trouble." I ask God to let us all experience double the manifestation of His power and miracles, compared to the manifestation of evil and trouble—that we would discover what the enemy meant for evil, God is using for good.

MOM & DAD: Your prayers and legacy live on in me and my family.

BILL & JOANNE: Thank you for being the best in-laws a guy could ask for.

PASTOR ROB: Thanks for always having my back!

PASTOR CLARENCE: You have stood by me and my family through every possible season of life.

PAT SPRINGLE: This book simply wouldn't exist without you!

Just a few weeks prior to my car wreck, we celebrated our 25th wedding anniversary with Rob and Becca and Bill and JoAnne.

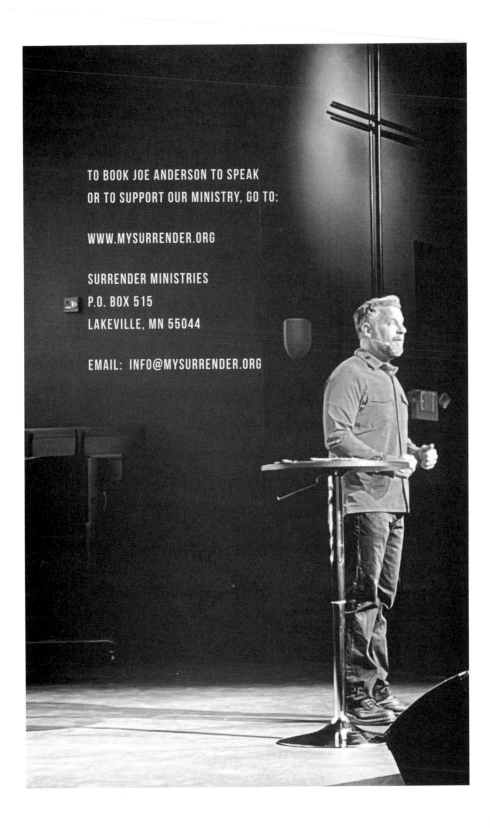

TO BOOK JOE ANDERSON TO SPEAK
OR TO SUPPORT OUR MINISTRY, GO TO:

WWW.MYSURRENDER.ORG

SURRENDER MINISTRIES
P.O. BOX 515
LAKEVILLE, MN 55044

EMAIL: INFO@MYSURRENDER.ORG

ORDER MORE COPIES

To order more copies of this book, go to
www.mysurrender.org or Amazon.com